SMOKE IT LIKE A

TEXAS

──★── PIT MASTER WITH YOUR ──★──

ELECTRIC SMOKER

SMOKE IT LIKE A

TEXAS

★ —— PIT MASTER WITH YOUR —— ★

ELECTRIC SMOKER

RECIPES & TECHNIQUES FOR BIGGER,
BOLDER LONE STAR FLAVOR

WENDY O'NEAL

Ulysses Press

Published by
Ulysses Press
P.O. Box 3440
Berkeley, CA 94703
www.ulyssespress.com

ISBN: 978-1-61243-789-7
Library of Congress Catalog Number 2018930776

Printed in the United States by Bang Printing

10 9 8 7 6 5 4 3 2 1

Acquisitions editor: Casie Vogel
Managing editor: Claire Chun
Project editor: Molly Conway
Editor: Shayna Keyles
Proofreader: Lauren Harrison
Front cover design: Raquel Castro
Interior design/layout: what!design @ whatweb.com
Photographs: © Wendy O'Neal except on pages 8 and 128 © Kate Eschbach

Distributed by Publishers Group West

John: Thank you for your unending support
and encouragement. And for always doing the dishes.

Contents

West Texas–Style Barbecue **91**

Desserts **119**

Conversion Charts **127**

About the Author **128**

INTRODUCTION

I was born and raised in Texas, until upper elementary school. I was born in Corpus Christi and lived there until we moved to Amarillo, in the Panhandle, when I was little girl. I lived for summers at my Granny and Bobo's lake house in North Texas. Even after we moved to Arizona, I loved going back every summer and visiting my cousins and extended family, eating barbecue and chicken-fried steak, watching rodeos and tractor pulls, and skiing on Lake Arrowhead.

Shortly after I married my husband, I bought him a $50 charcoal smoker and a smoker cookbook, and he's been in love ever since. We've had cheap smokers, expensive smokers, charcoal smokers, every type of smoker—but my favorite is a good-quality electric smoker. An electric smoker is perfect for hobby cooking. It's easy to use and doesn't require a lot of fuss during the cooking process.

I'm a self-taught cook, but I was given a great foundation in outdoor cooking by my dad and in the kitchen by my mom and my Granny. I remember watching cooking shows on PBS when I'd get home from school and writing down the recipes as the chefs cooked. I loved learning about new cuisines and discovering kitchen tips, so when the Food Network started, I was in heaven. I couldn't get enough! I had no desire to become a chef; I just wanted to be able to feed my family good food. The kitchen is the heart of the home, and I love bringing family and friends together over a delicious meal.

About Electric Smoking

Over the years, I've used both electric and charcoal smokers. While some people swear by charcoal smokers, they take a lot of patience and attention. That was perfect for me when I didn't have kids and could sit around watching the meat cook. Charcoal smokers require a more hands-on approach, and more skills and technique. They are standard in traditional Texas barbecue joints.

However, for the last fifteen years or so, I've used only electric smokers, and I must tell you that I prefer them. It's almost a set-it-and-forget-it sort of cooking, though you still need to add wood chips or baste your meat occasionally. The taste is pretty much the same, because the fact is that it's the wood chips that infuse the meats with flavor, not necessarily the charcoal. Texas barbecue can be easily made at home with an electric smoker, and it's still mouth-wateringly delicious.

Smoking is a low-and-slow cooking process, very different from grilling. Smoking temperatures are usually between 200°F to 275°F, compared to the high heat typically used for grilling (over 400°F). Smoking uses low heat and the meat is generally farther away from the heat source, resulting in a much longer cooking time.

Cooking times will vary slightly according to the size, shape, and cut of the meat and how often you open the smoker door to check in. Opening the door lets out heat and the electric smoker must come back up to the programmed temperature after the door is closed, which increases cooking time.

Smoking isn't just limited to meat—vegetables, breads, desserts, nuts, and even cheese are great in the smoker too. However, Texas barbecue is pretty much limited to beef, pork, and chicken.

Electric Smoker Features

Buying an electric smoker doesn't have to be scary or cost a fortune. There are good-quality electric smokers available for around $200. I've used different brands and models over the years, and I've found Masterbuilt and Char-Broil smokers to be of good quality and affordable. For me, I prefer a Masterbuilt Digital Electric Smoker. Other well-known brands include Bradley, Smoke Hollow, and Smokehouse.

Electric smokers are vertical smokers with multiple shelves that allow you to cook a lot of food at once. Get a smoker with the largest cooking capacity that you can afford. That way you'll be able to smoke multiple things all at once and not be limited by space. Here are some options to consider when purchasing your electric smoker:

Glass door vs. solid door. Glass doors look great on the showroom floor and in pictures online, but my experience is that after a couple of uses, the smoke buildup on the glass is so thick that you can't see through it.

Digital vs. analog. Both are great. An analog electric smoker has fewer parts to malfunction, but digital allows for setting precise temperatures and cooking times. If a digital smoker is in your future, get one that also has a remote control. That way, if the controls on the unit happen to malfunction, you can just use the remote. Plus, you can check temperatures and times from the comfort of your home.

Stands or legs. These are more of a luxury than a necessity. They raise the smoker off the ground for easier access and they allow for air circulation under the smoker. Both can be purchased aftermarket if you decide you want them.

Temperature probe. Again, this isn't necessary, but a good probe will help take the guesswork out of deciding when the food is fully cooked. This item can also be purchased aftermarket.

Before You Smoke

Most electric smokers come fully assembled, unless they have a stand or legs. After you've removed all the packaging and cleaned the racks, trays, and pans with soap and water, you'll need to season the smoker before you begin using it for food. Seasoning the smoker burns off any chemicals, grease, metal shavings, cardboard, or residues from the manufacturing and packaging process. This process also seals the smoker and bakes on the paint.

Seasoning times vary according to the brand and model, so refer to your specific electric smoker's user manual. For my Masterbuilt, the instructions say to heat the smoker to 275°F for 3 hours with a dry water pan in place, adding wood chips once during the last 45 minutes. Then, turn off the smoker and let it cool completely. Some smokers require you to rub a light layer of oil inside the smoker before seasoning it.

Must-Have Tools

Other than a good cooker, there aren't a ton of accessories used in Texas barbecue—all that's needed are some meat, wood chips, and a smoker. However, there are few accessories that are just plain fun or useful to have. Many of these can be found at big box and home improvement stores, online, and anywhere smokers are sold.

High-temperature gloves. Gloves or heavy-duty potholders are an absolute necessity. The smoker gets extremely hot, and removing food and trays can be tricky.

Cast-iron cookware. Cast iron heats evenly and is meant to take the abuse that smoking can inflict on pots and pans. I recommend having a couple different sizes, but measure before buying to make sure they will fit inside your smoker. I suggest having a 10-inch skillet, 8-inch skillet, and a 6- or 8-quart covered Dutch oven on hand.

Long-handled basting brushes or barbecue mops. The last thing you want to do is to reach your arm to the back of a hot smoker to baste your meat. Long-handled brushes or basting mops are a must!

Shredding claws. Yes, a pair of forks will work to shred pork or beef, but shredding claws make this task so easy! They are essential for any pit master.

Instant-read thermometer. You'll want a good thermometer for meats that need to be cooked to specific temperatures, such as prime rib and pulled pork. Some heat-resistant models can be inserted for the entire cooking time and will alert you when your meat reaches the target temperature. Others are inserted near the end of the cooking session to check the temperature.

Grill baskets. A few good grill baskets will keep smaller items together and keep food from falling through the slots in the smoker racks.

Disposable foil trays. I love using disposable foil trays whenever possible. They come in all shapes and sizes and are usually found in the baking or food storage section of the grocery store. These aren't necessary, but I don't want my good pots and pans to end up covered with a layer of smoke. Plus, disposables make for quick and easy cleanup. An 8 x 12-inch disposable foil pan is the size I use most.

Standing chicken roaster. A vertical roaster is a fun gadget to keep on hand. You can use it in the smoker, on the grill, or in the oven to cook a bird upright. Most versions have a place where you can add a can to make beer-can or soda-can chicken dinners. Cooking chicken vertically helps to keep it moist and allows the skin to crisp up evenly.

Meat injector. Many cooks like to inject their meats with liquid solutions to add flavor and keep the meat juicy. You'll need a good-quality injector for recipes that call for this.

Wood Chips

	Wood Type	Use with
	Alder	fish; good all-purpose chip
	Apple	chicken, pork, vegetables, desserts
	Cherry	chicken, pork, beef, desserts
	Hickory	good all-purpose chip
	Maple	pork, beef, vegetables, desserts
	Mesquite	good all-purpose chip
	Oak	beef, fish
	Pecan	chicken, pork, beef, vegetables

Each style of Texas barbecue typically uses a different type of wood. Central Texas uses oak and occasionally pecan (and sometimes mixes them together). East Texas uses hickory wood. South and West Texas both use mesquite.

It's a good idea to keep a wide selection of wood chips on hand for your smoker, since different types of wood impart different flavors to food. Soaking wood chips makes them burn longer and gives a less intense smoke flavor to your food. Dry wood chips burn more quickly and produce a more intense flavor. Both are totally fine—it's a matter of personal preference—though I personally recommend soaking chips for about 30 minutes and then draining a handful before placing them in the smoker, following your smoker's guidelines. Adding wood chips throughout the cooking time imparts wonderful, deep flavor. If you have unused soaked wood chips at the end of a smoking day, you don't need to toss them. Just dump out the water, let the chips dry completely, and return them to their storage bag.

Even though Texas barbecue only uses three or four types of wood, it's still good to have a variety of wood available in case you want to get creative or cook something other than Texas barbecue.

7 Easy Steps for Smoking Meat

1. Apply a dry or wet rub to the meat, place it in a large zip-top bag or covered dish, and let it marinate in the refrigerator overnight.

2. Add hot tap water to the water pan so that it's about three-quarters full. The amount of water depends on how big your smoker's water pan is; refer to your manufacturer's instructions for best results. (During long smoking sessions, you may need to add more liquid to keep it at that level.) You can also add seasonings, vegetables, or marinades to the water to add flavor during the cooking process.

3. Preheat your electric smoker. Once the smoker is hot, add food and then a handful of wood chips to the chip loading area. Use the damper on your smoker to adjust the amount of smoke.

4. If you're using a wet rub, pat your meat dry with paper towels before putting it in the smoker. (Any liquid marinades or sauces will burn, so save those for the last 30 minutes.) Place the meat in the smoker, leaving a little room all around to allow air to flow freely, but try to position the meat directly over the water pan so that any drippings will fall into the pan. You'll only need to turn the meat once or twice during the cooking cycle.

5. Maintain the smoker at the desired temperature. Adjusting the damper not only changes the amount of smoke, but can help regulate the temperature. Wood chips can be added as suggested for whatever you're cooking—but keep the door closed as much of the time as possible so that heat doesn't escape, extending the cooking time.

6. During the final 1 to 2 hours, you can baste your meat with a mop sauce or apply your barbecue sauce every 30 minutes.

7. Use a meat thermometer to determine when your meat is cooked to the proper temperature. Once it's at the proper temperature, remove the meat from the smoker and let it rest for 15 to 30 minutes tented loosely with foil to allow the juices to be redistributed, then slice or shred it. Resting applies to most meats; however, fish and seafood are usually served immediately. When you cut into to the meat, you may notice a red ring around the outside. This is the smoke ring and is highly desirable—it doesn't mean the meat is undercooked.

General Smoking Guidelines

Meat	Smoking Temperature	Time to Complete	Finished Temperature	Wood Chips
Beef brisket	225°F	1½ hrs/pound	190°F (sliced) 200°F (pulled)	Any
Beef ribs	225°F	3–4 hrs	175°F	Pecan
Pork butt	225°F	1½ hrs/pound	180°F (sliced) 205°F + until tender (pulled)	Cherry
Pork ribs, baby back	225°F–240°F	5–6 hrs	145°F + until tender	Cherry, Hickory
Whole chicken	250°F	4 hrs	165°F	Mesquite
Whole turkey (12 pounds)	240°F	6½ hrs	165°F	Hickory, Mesquite
Turkey breast (bone-in)	240°F	4–6 hrs	165°F	Hickory, Mesquite
Salmon, steaks or fillets	140°F–160°F	5–7 hrs	145°F	Hickory

Cleaning and Maintenance

Clean the smoker's drip pans and trays after every smoking session, but wait for the smoker to completely cool down first. (I usually wait until the next day, since I generally use my smoker to cook supper. Letting it sit overnight ensures that it's completely cool.)

Empty the drippings from the water pan into a disposable cup, a doubled plastic bag, or anything that can be sealed and thrown into the trash. *Do not* dump the drippings down the sink, because over time this could lead to a clogged drain. After emptying the water pan, remove all the smoker's racks and pans and clean them with regular dishwashing soap and hot water. Dry completely and return them to the smoker.

There's usually no need to clean the inside walls of the smoker. The black soot that builds up on the inside actually gives off a ton of flavor. In all my years of smoking, I've never had to clean the inside of a smoker. However, that doesn't mean there aren't occasions when it might be necessary. In rare circumstances, you might need to clean the inside if something was spilled or bugs have gotten inside. However, don't use harsh chemicals, but rather a 50/50 blend of white vinegar and hot water to wipe down the smoker with a soft sponge (only after the smoker has completely cooled and been unplugged). The soot will come off the inside walls when you clean them, so you'll need to re-season your smoker before cooking again.

The best way to keep the outside of your smoker clean is to cover it when it's not in use. Covers can be purchased online, at home improvement stores, or wherever smokers are sold. Having a good cover protects the electronics too.

Safety

With an electric smoker, there isn't an open flame or hot coals to worry about, but there are still safety precautions that need to be taken. Smokers get *hot*, and even the slightest touch can result in a burn. Heavy-duty tongs and potholders are necessities for every grill master. Keep kids and pets away from the electric smoker, as even the outside of the unit will become extremely hot.

It's important to protect your smoker from extreme weather (rain, snow, intense sun) to safeguard its electronic components. My smoker has had its share of blown fuses when the power cord got wet, even when it wasn't in use. I keep my electric smoker under our patio roof, but as close to the edge as possible. This keeps it out of the elements but away from the house, and it provides a quick escape route for the smoke.

Be sure to read your owner's manual for specific details about the electric cooker model that you are using.

CENTRAL TEXAS-STYLE BARBECUE

Central Texas barbecue is what most people think of when they think of Texas-style barbecue. It was founded by German and other European immigrants who owned meat-packing plants in the area. They then opened meat markets that served cooked meat wrapped in butcher paper. Today, you'll find Central Texas–style barbecue served on a tray lined with butcher paper (you won't find any sandwiches here) and just a few simple sides like sliced white onion, pickles, white bread, and usually an RC Cola.

What makes this style of barbecue stand out is the simplicity of preparation. You won't find fancy rubs or sauces, just good meat with a simple blend of black pepper, salt, and occasionally some garlic powder. Oak is the wood of choice for smoking since it's native to the area, but occasionally pecan wood is used, either alone or in addition to the oak.

CENTRAL TEXAS CLASSIC RUB

All that's needed for delicious, classic Texas barbecue is freshly ground black pepper and kosher salt! Some say that the ideal proportion is 5:1 pepper to salt, but I've found a 2:1 or 3:1 ratio is ideal for most home smoking recipes.

Prep time: 5 minutes   *Makes:* 1½ cups

1 cup coarsely ground black pepper

½ cup coarse kosher salt

Combine the salt and pepper in bowl. Store in an airtight container for up to 6 months.

Note: Since the only ingredients for this rub are salt and pepper, splurge for a good-quality pepper that is coarsely ground. Don't buy the pre-ground black pepper from the can in the grocery store; it's not the same. If you can't find a good-quality, fresh, coarsely ground black pepper, try buying whole peppercorns and grinding them in a coffee grinder.

SIMPLE TEXAS BBQ SAUCE

While classic Central Texas barbecue doesn't typically use a sauce, many people are accustomed to some sort of sauce for their barbecue. You'll find this very simple, thin sauce with no sweetener to be a good accompaniment to Central Texas–style barbecue.

Prep time: 5 minutes   *Cook time:* 30 minutes   *Makes:* about 1½ cups

1 (8-ounce) can tomato sauce

2 cups (16 ounces) water

1 tablespoon apple cider vinegar

4 teaspoons chili powder

1 teaspoon garlic powder

pinch of coarse kosher salt

In a small saucepan over medium-high heat, add all ingredients and whisk to combine. Bring to a boil, then lower heat to a simmer. Simmer until barbecue sauce is reduced by about half, or about 30 minutes.

CENTRAL TEXAS-STYLE BRISKET

Central Texas–style brisket is dark, peppery, and the star of all Texas barbecue. There are no fancy sauces or rubs to hide behind; the meat really must stand on its own. Buy the best black pepper or freshly grind it yourself. Just try to stay away from the pre-ground black pepper from the spice aisle in the grocery store.

Prep time: 15 minutes   *Smoke time:* 8–9 hours   *Wood chips:* Oak   *Serves:* 10–12

5–6 pounds trimmed beef brisket

6 tablespoons coarsely ground black pepper

3 tablespoons coarse kosher salt

white bread, sliced pickles, and white onions, for serving

1. Prepare the smoker's water pan according to the manufacturer's instructions and preheat the smoker to 225°F. While it heats, fill a medium bowl with water and add 3 or 4 handfuls of oak wood chips to soak.

2. Remove the brisket from its wrapping, dry with paper towels, and trim any remaining fat. In a small bowl, combine the pepper and salt. Rub the mixture over the brisket, making sure the meat is heavily covered.

3. Place the brisket in the smoker and add a small handful of the soaked wood chips to the chip loading area. Add more chips at least every 30 minutes. Smoke for 4–6 hours, or until the internal temperature of the meat is 165°F.

4. Remove the brisket from the smoker, wrap tightly in parchment paper, and return to the smoker for another 2–3 hours. Do not add wood chips during this time, as no more smoke will penetrate the meat.

5. Remove from smoker and let rest for 30 minutes under a foil tent. Slice the meat into thin slices, making sure to slice against the grain of the meat.

6. Serve on top of white bread with a side of sliced pickles and white onions.

Getting the Smoke Ring

Oh, the smoke ring! Everyone wants to have it on their smoked meat; however, it's virtually impossible to get using an electric smoker. The red smoke ring is a chemical reaction that occurs between a protein in meat called myoglobin and the gases nitric oxide (NO) and carbon monoxide (CO). NO and CO are made by carbon and nitrogen combining with oxygen during the combustion of wood or charcoal. The actual smoke really has nothing to do with it, and because of the need for wood or charcoal, it just doesn't happen naturally with an electric smoker. The good news is that the smoke ring doesn't change any flavors or have its own flavor; it simply adds a beautiful visual to the meat.

There is a way to fake the smoke ring, though! This is a total cheater method and not required or needed for delicious barbecue. But if you really want that smoke ring, try this technique:

When preparing the meat, use about ½ teaspoon of pink curing salt. Sprinkle the curing salt all over the trimmed meat in a very thin layer. Gently rub the salt around and let it sit for about 2–3 minutes. Rinse off the meat (very important, because the pink curing salt is not edible), pat dry, and add any rub or seasonings as normal. Place the meat in a cold smoker and then turn on the smoker to the desired temperature. Note that if you are cooking a large piece of meat, this method is not recommended, as the amount of time that the meat is in the unsafe temperature zone could lead to food-borne illnesses.

LEMON PEPPER CHICKEN QUARTERS

Backyard barbecues will never be the same again once you start making this chicken. I love making this recipe with just legs and thighs. The addition of lemon pepper really gives the chicken a great flavor. Move over barbecue sauce, hello lemon pepper!

Prep time: 15 minutes *Smoke time:* 2½–3 hours *Wood chips:* Oak *Serves:* 4

4 chicken quarters, bone in, skin on, about 6 pounds

2 tablespoons olive oil

2 teaspoons coarse kosher salt

2 teaspoons lemon pepper

1 teaspoon garlic powder

1 teaspoon chili powder

1 teaspoon coarsely ground black pepper

½ teaspoon ground cumin

1. Prepare the smoker's water pan according to the manufacturer's instructions and preheat the smoker to 225°F. While it heats, fill a medium bowl with water and add 2 to 3 handfuls of wood chips to soak.

2. Remove the chicken pieces from packaging and pat dry. Gently coat each piece with ½ tablespoon of olive oil. Combine remaining ingredients in a small bowl and rub each piece of chicken with the seasonings until well coated.

3. Place chicken directly onto the smoking rack, skin side up. Add a small handful of the soaked wood chips to the chip loading area, and keep adding more chips at least every 30 minutes. The chicken is done when it reaches an internal temperature of 165°F, after 2½–3 hours. Remove from the smoker and serve while hot.

PEPPERED TURKEY BREAST

Don't wait until Thanksgiving to make this turkey. The coarsely ground black pepper gives the turkey a little kick and makes it a delicious addition to sandwiches all year long. If you have a large enough smoker to handle a whole 12–14-pound turkey, then double the oil and rub, and prepare as directed below. Increase cooking time to 6–8 hours (plan 25–30 minutes per pound).

Prep time: 15 minutes   *Smoke time:* 3½–4½ hours   *Wood chips:* Oak   *Serves:* 4–6

1 (6–8-pound) whole turkey breast, bone-in

2 teaspoons coarsely ground black pepper

1 teaspoon coarse kosher salt

½ teaspoon chili powder

½ teaspoon ground cumin

¼ teaspoon garlic powder

1–2 tablespoons olive oil

1. Prepare the smoker's water pan according to the manufacturer's instructions and preheat the electric smoker to 250°F. While it heats, fill a medium bowl with water and add 3 or 4 handfuls of wood chips to soak.

2. Remove any turkey giblets from the cavity of the bird, then rinse and dry well. In a medium bowl, combine the dry seasonings and stir with a fork to combine. Generously rub olive oil on all sides of the breast, including the inside. Rub the dry seasoning all over the breast and inside the cavity as well. You should use all the rub. Add some under any loose skin for even more flavor.

3. Set the turkey breast directly on a smoker rack, breast side up, and add a small handful of the soaked wood chips to the chip loading area. Keep adding more chips at least every 30 minutes. The turkey is done when it reaches an internal temperature of 165°F, 3½–4½ hours, depending on the size of your turkey breast.

4. Remove from smoker and loosely place a foil tent over the breast. Let it rest for 15–30 minutes before slicing.

LEMON GARLIC PORK TENDERLOIN

Kick up a boring pork tenderloin with the flavors of lemon and garlic for a delicious supper the whole family will love.

Prep time: 15 minutes   *Smoke time:* 2–2½ hours   *Wood chips:* Oak   *Serves:* 3–4

1 small (1½–2-pound) pork tenderloin

1 teaspoon coarse kosher salt

1 teaspoon lemon pepper

½ teaspoon garlic powder

½ teaspoon chili powder

½ teaspoon coarsely ground black pepper

1. Prepare the smoker's water pan according to the manufacturer's instructions and preheat the smoker to 225°F. While it heats, fill a medium bowl with water and add a couple handfuls of wood chips to soak.

2. Dry the tenderloin with paper towels. In a small bowl, add seasonings and stir to combine.

3. Place the tenderloin directly on the smoker rack and add a small handful of the soaked chips to the chip loading area. Adding more chips at least every 30 minutes, cook the tenderloin until the internal temperature has reached 155°F, 2–2½ hours.

4. Let the tenderloin rest under a foil tent for 15–20 minutes before slicing.

INCREDIBLE TEXAS-STYLE BABY BACK RIBS

Ribs should not be "fall off the bone" tender, but should have a little bite to them. These ribs are perfect and so full of flavor that no sauce is needed. If your smoker won't hold an entire rack, just cut the ribs into half-rack portions to smoke them.

Prep time: 20 minutes, plus 1 hour to marinate   *Smoke time:* 3½–4 hours   *Wood chips:* Oak and pecan   *Serves:* 3–4

2 teaspoons coarsely ground black pepper

2 teaspoon coarse kosher salt

1 teaspoon chili powder

1 teaspoon ground cumin

½ teaspoon garlic powder

½ teaspoon cayenne pepper

7–8 pounds (or 2 racks) baby back pork ribs

1 cup Simple Texas BBQ Sauce (page 21) (optional)

1. Combine black pepper, salt, chili powder, cumin, garlic, and cayenne pepper in a small bowl and set aside. Prepare the ribs by removing the thin membrane from the back side (see below). Pat the ribs dry with a paper towel and liberally apply the prepared rub all over, including the ends and side pieces. Place the ribs in a large zip-top plastic bag and refrigerate for 1 hour.

2. Prepare the smoker's water pan according to the manufacturer's instructions and preheat the smoker to 225°F. While it heats, fill a medium bowl with water and add 3 or 4 handfuls of wood chips to soak. Soak an equal amount of pecan and oak chips together.

3. Use tongs to remove the ribs from the bag and place them directly on the smoker racks, meat side facing up. Add a small handful of the soaked wood chips to the chip loading area, and keep adding more chips at least every 30 minutes. Smoke the ribs for 4–5 hours, until the bones start to show and the meat is tender but not falling off the bone.

4. Let the ribs rest for 15 minutes under a foil tent, cut apart to serve, and serve with Simple Texas BBQ Sauce, if desired.

Removing the membrane

Removing the thin membrane from the back side of baby back ribs can be tricky, but it's well worth the effort. Not only does it make the ribs more tender and easier to eat, but it also allows the rub and any sauce to be absorbed on both sides of the ribs.

Use the tip of a sharp knife to pierce the membrane and begin to separate it from the ribs. Grab the membrane with a paper towel and pull it away from the entire rack of ribs.

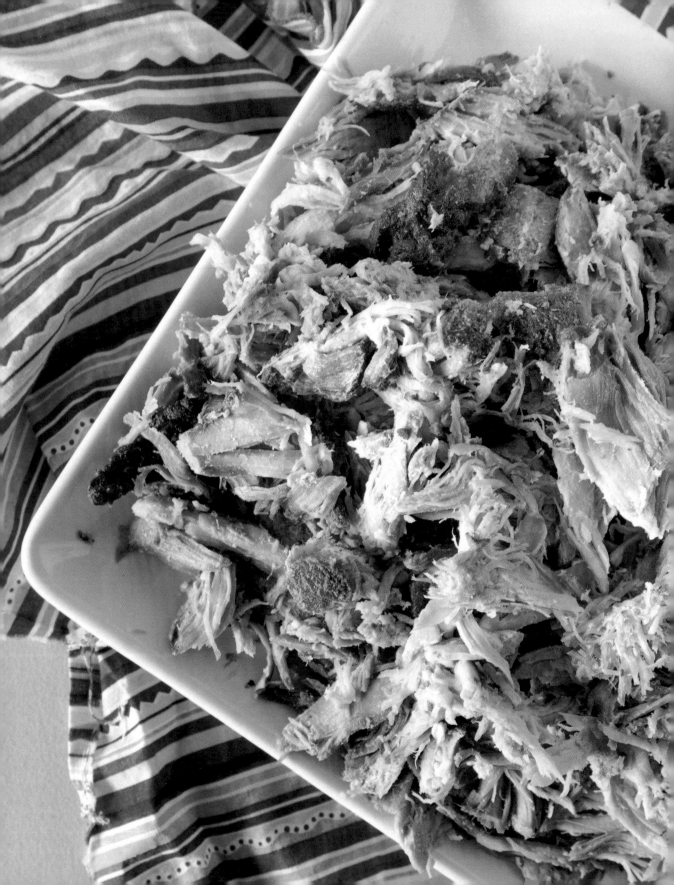

APPLE CIDER VINEGAR PULLED PORK

This pulled pork is my absolute favorite, yet it's so simple to make. The apple cider mop adds color, flavor, and moisture, and helps create the bark on the outside, which adds delicious taste and texture to the pork. Serve on a plate or on a bun. Either way, it makes enough to feed a hungry crowd.

Prep time: 30 minutes   *Smoke time:* 10–12 hours   *Wood chips:* Pecan and oak   *Serves:* 20

7 pounds pork butt (shoulder)

4 tablespoons coarse kosher salt

4 tablespoons coarsely ground black pepper

2 tablespoons garlic powder

1 cup apple cider vinegar

2 tablespoons brown sugar

½ teaspoon cayenne pepper

1–2 cups Simple Texas BBQ Sauce (page 21)

1. Prepare the smoker's water pan according to the manufacturer's instructions and preheat the smoker to 230°F. While it heats, fill a medium bowl with water and add 3 or 4 handfuls of wood chips to soak. Soak an equal amount of pecan and oak chips together.

2. Remove the pork butt from its packaging and trim off any large pieces of fat. Pat dry and set aside. Combine salt, black pepper, and garlic powder in a small bowl and apply liberally to prepared pork butt.

3. Place the pork in the smoker and add a small handful of the soaked wood chips to the chip loading area. Add more chips at least every 30 minutes.

4. Meanwhile, in a small saucepan over medium-high heat, combine apple cider vinegar, brown sugar, and cayenne pepper. Bring to low boil and lower heat to a simmer. Reduce the mixture by about half. Use this mixture on a mop to brush on the pork every 30 minutes, when adding wood chips.

5. After 6 hours of smoking, remove pork from smoker and wrap in heavy-duty foil. Return to the smoker for an additional 4–6 hours. Do not add any more wood chips after the pork is wrapped. The pork is done when it shreds easily with two forks.

6. Remove from smoker and let pork rest under a foil tent for 10–20 minutes before shredding. Add some Simple Texas BBQ Sauce to the shredded pork for serving.

PEPPERED PORK SPARE RIBS

Spare ribs often have less meat than baby back ribs, but their mix of meat and fat make them delicious and a great option for low and slow smoking.

Prep time: 15 minutes, plus 1 hour to marinate   *Smoke time:* 3½–4 hours   *Wood chips:* Oak
Serves: 4

3 tablespoons coarsely ground black pepper

1 tablespoon coarse kosher salt

1 tablespoon garlic powder

2½–3 pounds pork spare ribs

1 cup Simple Texas BBQ Sauce (page 21) (optional)

1. Combine black pepper, salt, and garlic powder in a small bowl and set aside. Prepare the ribs by removing the thin membrane from the back side (see page 31). Pat the ribs dry with a paper towel and liberally apply the prepared rub all over, including the ends and side pieces. Place the ribs in a large zip-top plastic bag and refrigerate for 1 hour.

2. Prepare the smoker's water pan according to the manufacturer's instructions and preheat the smoker to 225°F. While it heats, fill a medium bowl with water and add 3 or 4 handfuls of wood chips to soak.

3. Use tongs to remove the ribs from the bag and place them directly on the smoker racks, meat side facing up. Add a small handful of the soaked wood chips to the chip loading area, and add more chips at least every 30 minutes. Smoke the ribs for 3½–4 hours, until the bones start to show and the meat is tender but not falling off the bone.

4. Let ribs rest for 15 minutes under a foil tent, cut apart to serve, and serve with Simple Texas BBQ Sauce, if desired.

TENDER BONE-IN BEEF SHORT RIBS

Impress your family and friends with a rack of these huge beef short ribs! Using simple ingredients will let the sweetness of the meat shine through. Beef is king in Texas—let it speak for itself!

Prep time: 30 minutes   *Smoke time:* 3–8 hours   *Wood chips:* Pecan and oak   *Serves:* 4–6

¼ cup coarse kosher salt

¼ cup coarsely ground black pepper

¼ cup garlic powder

1 rack (4–5 pounds) beef short ribs

1. Combine black pepper, salt, and garlic powder in a small bowl and set aside. Cut ribs into 2-rib sections, which will help them cook faster and more evenly. Pat the ribs dry with a paper towel and liberally apply the prepared rub all over, including the ends and side pieces.

2. Prepare the smoker's water pan according to the manufacturer's instructions and preheat the smoker to 225°F. While it heats, fill a medium bowl with water and add 3 or 4 handfuls of wood chips to soak. Soak an equal amount of pecan and oak chips together.

3. Place ribs directly on the smoker racks, meat side facing up. Add a small handful of the soaked wood chips to the chip loading area, and keep adding more chips at least every 30 minutes. Once the ribs reach a temperature of 165°F (start checking for this temperature around the 2-hour mark), remove them from the smoker, and wrap in butcher paper.

4. Return ribs to smoker until internal temperature reaches 185°F and the meat is tender, but not falling off the bone. Do not add wood chips after ribs are wrapped since the smoke cannot penetrate the butcher paper. (Note: Beef short ribs can take up to 8 hours or longer depending on the size of the ribs and how much meat is on them.)

5. Let rest for 15 minutes under a foil tent, then cut ribs apart to serve.

BEEF SHOULDER ROAST

Beef shoulder (also known as beef clod) isn't cooked a lot at home, but it was a huge part of Central Texas barbecue history. It used to be served in a lot of smokehouses before brisket took over in popularity. Today, some smokehouses still smoke it and occasionally label it as lean brisket, despite it coming from the shoulder and not the chest as brisket does. It should be cooked well-done; it will have a similar taste and appearance to a pot roast.

Prep time: 15 minutes   *Smoke time:* 3–4 hours   *Wood chips:* Oak   *Serves:* 6–8

2 tablespoons coarse kosher salt

2 tablespoons coarsely ground black pepper

1 tablespoon cayenne pepper

3 pounds beef shoulder (clod) roast

1–2 cups Simple Texas BBQ Sauce (page 21)

1. Combine black pepper, salt, and cayenne powder in a small bowl and liberally apply the prepared rub all over the roast.

2. Prepare the smoker's water pan according to the manufacturer's instructions and preheat the smoker to 225°F. While it heats, fill a medium bowl with water and add 3 or 4 handfuls of wood chips to soak.

3. Place shoulder directly on racks, fat side up, and smoke for 3–4 hours. Add a small handful of the soaked wood chips to the chip loading area, and keep adding more chips at least every 30 minutes until the shoulder is tender and has an internal temperature of 200°F. When smoking below 250°F as in this recipe, plan for about 1 hour for every pound of meat.

4. Remove the shoulder from the smoker and let it rest under a foil tent for 10–15 minutes before slicing. Serve with a little bit of Simple Texas BBQ Sauce.

Note: If smoking the whole shoulder, consider smoking overnight or plan for all day, because a whole shoulder can weight around 25 pounds.

STUFFED CORNISH GAME HENS

Fancy enough for a holiday meal or party, but simple enough for a weeknight supper!

Prep time: 55 minutes   *Smoke time:* 1½–2 hours   *Wood chips:* Pecan   *Serves:* 4

¼ cup minced onion

½ cup chopped celery

1 tablespoon minced garlic

½ cup (1 stick) butter

1 tablespoon plus 1 teaspoon coarse kosher salt, divided

¾ teaspoon ground sage

½ teaspoon dried thyme

¼ teaspoon coarsely ground black pepper

4½ cups soft bread cubes

1 tablespoon poultry seasoning

2 teaspoon garlic powder

1 teaspoon paprika

4 Cornish game hens

2 tablespoons extra virgin olive oil

1. In a large skillet, cook the onion, celery, and garlic in butter over medium-high heat until the vegetables are tender, 10–15 minutes. Mix in 1 teaspoon of the salt and the sage, thyme, and pepper. Turn off the heat, gently stir in the bread cubes, and set aside.

2. Prepare the smoker's water pan according to the manufacturer's instructions and preheat the smoker to 275°F. While it heats, fill a medium bowl with water and add 3 or 4 handfuls of wood chips to soak.

3. Combine remaining salt, poultry seasoning, garlic powder, and paprika in a small bowl and set aside. Remove the birds from packaging and remove any giblets (there usually aren't any, but always double check). Rinse the birds and pat dry. Rub ½ tablespoon of olive oil on each bird and sprinkle liberally with prepared rub.

4. Stuff each bird with about ½ cup of dressing, or until the cavity is filled completely. Tie the legs with baker's twine to hold the legs together and to keep the stuffing from falling out. Place the birds in smoker, breast side down. Add a small handful of the soaked wood chips to the chip loading area, and keep adding more chips at least every 30 minutes until the Cornish game hens are done, 1½–2 hours. Both the chicken and stuffing should have an internal temperature of 165°F.

EAST TEXAS-STYLE BARBECUE

East Texas–style barbecue might be the exact opposite of Central style. It is fall-off-the-bone tender meat, smoked over hickory wood, and served with a sweet tomato-based barbecue sauce.

This style of barbecue has been influenced by Southern Black communities and the neighboring flavors of Louisiana. Rubs and sauces are heavy, sweet, and almost always include brown sugar. You'll have brisket served chopped and on a bun with a selection of delicious sides like coleslaw, beans, potato salad, fried okra, and mac and cheese.

EAST TEXAS BBQ RUB

Mix up this rub in large batches and use it liberally on beef, chicken, pork, or even fish.

Prep time: 5 minutes   *Makes:* about ½ cup

4 tablespoons light brown sugar

2 tablespoons coarsely ground black pepper

2 tablespoons coarse kosher salt

2 teaspoons garlic powder

1 teaspoon cayenne powder

Combine all the rub ingredients in an airtight container, stirring to mix well. For easy barbecue, double or triple this recipe and store in a cool, dark place for up to 6 months.

EAST TEXAS BBQ SAUCE

This simple, classic barbecue sauce is lightly sweet and easy to make. It's the perfect addition to anything coming off the smoker or even the grill.

Prep time: 5 minutes   *Cook time:* 20 minutes   *Makes:* about 2 cups

2 (8-ounce) cans tomato sauce

¼ cup brown sugar

3 teaspoons apple cider vinegar

2 teaspoons Worcestershire sauce

2 teaspoons garlic powder

1 teaspoon dry mustard

½ teaspoon coarse kosher salt

In a medium saucepan, combine all ingredients over medium-high heat. Stir often and bring to a boil. Reduce heat and simmer 15–20 minutes. Pour into a mason jar with a lid and store in the refrigerator for up to a week. Serve warm, cold, or room temperature.

SAUCY CHOPPED BRISKET

For the perfect East Texas–inspired supper, serve this hickory-smoked chopped brisket on a hamburger bun with plenty of Mustard Potato Salad (recipe follows).

Prep time: 15 minutes   *Smoke time:* 8–9 hours   *Wood chips:* Hickory   *Serves:* 10–12

5–6 pounds trimmed beef brisket

½ cup East Texas BBQ Rub
(page 45)

½–1 cup East Texas BBQ Sauce
(page 45)

1. Prepare the smoker's water pan according to the manufacturer's instructions and preheat the smoker to 225°F. While it heats, fill a medium bowl with water and add 3 or 4 handfuls of wood chips to soak.

2. Remove the brisket from its wrapping, dry with paper towels, and trim any remaining fat. Rub the East Texas BBQ Rub over the brisket, making sure to cover brisket heavily.

3. Place the brisket in the smoker and add a small handful of the soaked wood chips to the chip loading area. Add more chips at least every 30 minutes. Smoke the brisket for 5–6 hours, or until the internal temperature of the meat is 165°F.

4. Remove the brisket from the smoker, wrap tightly in parchment paper, and return to smoker for at least another 3 hours. Do not add wood chips the last few hours as no more smoke will penetrate the meat.

5. Remove from smoker and let rest with parchment paper on for 30 minutes. Remove parchment paper and chop brisket into ½ inch pieces (bite size), removing any large pieces of fat, and place into a large bowl. Stir in ½ cup (or more) barbecue sauce just until all the meat is lightly coated.

CLASSIC MUSTARD POTATO SALAD

½ cup finely diced sweet onions

¼ cup finely diced celery (about 2 stalks)

¼ cup finely diced dill pickles or dill pickle relish

½ cup mayonnaise

1 tablespoon prepared yellow mustard

1 tablespoon pickle juice

½ teaspoon coarse kosher salt

⅛ teaspoon coarsely ground black pepper

½ tablespoons sugar

2 cups peeled, cooked, and diced white potatoes

2 eggs, hard boiled and finely diced

1. In a large bowl, combine the onion, celery, pickles, mayonnaise, mustard, pickle juice, salt, pepper, and sugar. Stir well to combine. Gently fold in potatoes and eggs. Stir until well coated.

2. Cover and refrigerate at least 3 hours or up to overnight. Keep refrigerated until ready to serve.

SIMPLY PERFECT PORK SPARE RIBS

This is a great simple recipe for beginners. Just simple flavors and a no-fuss smoking technique create a delicious smoked rack of ribs. Serve with barbecue sauce, if desired, and a big helping of Jalapeño Coleslaw (recipe follows).

Prep time: 15 minutes, plus 1 hour to marinate   *Smoke time:* 4–5 hours   *Wood chips:* Hickory
Serves: 3–4

2½–3 pounds pork spare ribs

¼–½ cup East Texas BBQ Rub
(page 45)

1. Prepare the ribs by removing the thin membrane from the back side (see page 31). Pat the ribs dry with a paper towel and liberally apply the prepared rub all over, including the ends and side pieces. Place the ribs in a large zip-top plastic bag and refrigerate for 1 hour.

2. Prepare the smoker's water pan according to the manufacturer's instructions and preheat the smoker to 225°F. While it heats, fill a medium bowl with water and add 3 or 4 handfuls of wood chips to soak.

3. Use tongs to remove the ribs from the bag and place them directly on the smoker racks, meat side facing up. Add a small handful of the soaked wood chips to the chip loading area, and keep adding more chips at least every 30 minutes. Smoke the ribs for 4–5 hours, until the bones start to show and the meat is tender but not falling off the bone.

4. Let rest for 15 minutes under a foil tent, then cut ribs apart to serve.

JALAPEÑO COLESLAW

7 cups shredded cabbage

1 cup shredded carrots

1 (16-ounce) bottle coleslaw dressing

3 jalapeños, stems cut off

Combine cabbage and carrots in a large bowl. Puree jalapeños and pour into coleslaw dressing. Pour dressing over cabbage mixture, stir, cover, and refrigerate for several hours. Stir well before serving.

SWEET HICKORY PORK SHOULDER

The brown sugar in the rub, the sauce, and the apple juice in the water pan add a delicious hint of sweetness that make this pulled pork irresistible.

Prep time: 30 minutes   *Smoke time:* 10–12   *Wood chips:* Hickory   *Serves:* 20

½–1 cup apple juice

7½–8 pounds pork butt (shoulder)

½ cup East Texas BBQ Rub (page 45)

1 teaspoon onion powder

½ teaspoon chili powder

1–2 cups East Texas BBQ Sauce (page 45)

1. Prepare the smoker's water pan according to the manufacturer's instructions, adding equal amounts of apple juice and water to the pan, then preheat the smoker to 230°F. While it heats, fill a medium bowl with water and add 3 or 4 handfuls of wood chips to soak.

2. Remove pork butt from packaging and trim any large pieces of fat. Pat dry and set aside. Combine rub, onion powder, and chili powder in a small bowl and apply liberally to the pork butt.

3. Place the pork butt in the smoker and add a small handful of the soaked wood chips to the chip loading area. Add more chips at least every 30 minutes.

4. After 6 hours of smoking, remove pork from the smoker, wrap in heavy-duty foil, and return to smoker for an additional 4–6 hours. Do not add any more wood chips after the pork is wrapped. The pork is done when it shreds easily with two forks.

5. Remove from smoker and let the pork rest under a foil tent for 10–20 minutes before shredding. Serve on a hamburger bun with plenty of East Texas BBQ Sauce.

Note: Got leftovers? Try topping tortilla chips with some of this pulled pork, blue cheese crumbles, Pico de Gallo (page 81), and a little more barbecue sauce. Put everything on a baking sheet and heat at 350°F for 10–15 minutes for a delicious twist on nachos!

JALAPEÑO BBQ RIBS

One of my favorite ribs, these saucy baby backs aren't super spicy, but get a nice subtle heat from the jalapeños.

Prep time: 15 minutes   *Smoke time:* 3½–4½ hours   *Wood chips:* Hickory   *Serves:* 2–3

7–8 pounds (about 2 racks) baby back ribs

½ cup East Texas BBQ Rub (page 45)

½–1 cup East Texas BBQ Sauce (page 45)

4 jalapeños, sliced

1. Prepare the smoker's water pan according to the manufacturer's instructions and preheat the smoker to 225°F. While it heats, fill a medium bowl with water and add 3 or 4 handfuls of wood chips to soak.

2. Prepare the ribs by removing the thin membrane from the backside (see page 31). Pat the ribs dry with a paper towel and liberally apply the prepared rub all over, including the ends and side pieces.

3. Place the ribs directly on the smoker racks, meat side facing up. Add a small handful of the soaked wood chips to the chip loading area, and keep adding more chips at least every 30 minutes.

4. After 2½–3 hours, remove the ribs from the smoker and place them on large piece of foil. Liberally pour barbecue sauce over the ribs and top with sliced jalapeños. Wrap the ribs tightly in the foil and return to the smoker for another 1–1½ hours. Do not add any more wood chips after the pork is wrapped. Ribs are done when the bones start to show and the meat is tender but not falling off the bone.

5. Let the ribs rest in the foil for 15 minutes, then cut them apart. Serve with additional barbecue sauce, if desired.

SMOKED TURKEY LEGS

Sweet and spicy, these giant, fair-style turkey legs are even better than at the fair and will put a smile on kids' faces everywhere.

Prep time: 30 minutes, plus 12–24 hours to brine   *Smoke time:* 3–4 hours   *Wood chips:* Hickory   *Serves:* 6

FOR THE BRINE

½ cup table salt

½ cup brown sugar

2 tablespoons onion powder

2 tablespoons garlic powder

2 tablespoons red pepper flakes

2 tablespoons poultry seasoning

1 tablespoon Tabasco

2 bay leaves

¾–1 gallon water

6 large turkey legs

FOR THE RUB

2 tablespoons chili powder

2 teaspoons steak seasoning

2 teaspoons paprika

1 teaspoon onion powder

1 teaspoon garlic powder

1 teaspoon coarse kosher salt

olive oil

1. Mix all the brine ingredients in a large container with a lid and add turkey legs. Let turkey legs sit in brine for 12–24 hours, stirring occasionally.

2. Prepare the smoker's water pan according to the manufacturer's instructions and preheat the smoker to 250°F. While it heats, fill a medium bowl with water and add 3 or 4 handfuls of wood chips to soak.

3. Meanwhile, remove turkey legs from the brine, rinse, and pat dry. Mix rub ingredients together in a small bowl, except the olive oil. Lightly drizzle olive oil over the turkey legs, then sprinkle the rub over the legs and gently rub to coat.

4. Place turkey legs in the smoker and add a small handful of the soaked wood chips to the chip loading area. Add more chips at least every 30 minutes. Smoke for 3–4 hours, or until the internal temperature of the thickest part of the turkey leg is 165°F.

COCOA AND CHILI RUBBED PORK CHOPS

Add a little kick to your everyday pork chops by adding some unsweetened cocoa powder and chili powder. Serve with a green salad and big bowl of applesauce.

Prep time: 10 minutes   *Smoke time:* 45–60 minutes   *Wood chips:* Hickory   *Serves:* 4

1 tablespoon unsweetened cocoa powder

1 tablespoon brown sugar

1 tablespoon chili powder

¼ teaspoon ground cinnamon

1 teaspoon ground cumin

1 tablespoon coarse kosher salt

¼ teaspoon coarsely ground black pepper

4 bone-in pork chops

1. Prepare the smoker's water pan according to the manufacturer's instructions. Preheat the smoker to 275°F. While it heats, fill a medium bowl with water and add a handful of wood chips to soak.

2. In a small bowl, combine the unsweetened cocoa powder, brown sugar, chili powder, cinnamon, cumin, salt, and pepper. Sprinkle rub on both sides of the pork chops and place in the smoker. Add wood chips at the beginning of the cooking time only.

3. Check pork chops for doneness after smoking for 45 minutes. Pork will dry out quickly and shouldn't be overcooked. Total cook time will depend on how thick the pork chops are.

CAJUN PORK TENDERLOIN

East Texas borrows a lot of flavors from Louisiana, so a spicy Cajun-style pork tenderloin is a must-try. Getting the rub deep into the pork really gives the whole tenderloin a ton of flavor instead of just a smoky Cajun layer on the outside.

Prep time: 20 minutes   *Smoke time:* 2–2½ hours   *Wood chips:* Hickory   *Serves:* 2–4

1 (1½–2-pound) pork tenderloin

1 tablespoon butter, melted

½ teaspoon dried oregano

½ teaspoon dried thyme

½ teaspoon coarse kosher salt

¼ teaspoon cayenne

¼ teaspoon ground mustard

¼ teaspoon coarsely ground black pepper

1. Prepare the smoker's water pan according to the manufacturer's instructions and preheat the smoker to 235°F. While it heats, fill a medium bowl with water and add a couple handfuls of wood chips to soak.

2. Prepare the tenderloin by drying with paper towels. Using a sharp steak knife, cut 15–20 slits all over the tenderloin. Make the slits about ½ inch deep and about 1 inch wide. In a small bowl, combine remaining ingredients and stir to combine. Use a spoon to add this butter mixture to each of the slits and then rub the remaining mixture all over the outside of the tenderloin.

3. Place the tenderloin directly on the smoker rack and add a small handful of the soaked chips to the chip loading area. Adding more chips at least every 30 minutes, cook the tenderloin until the internal temperature has reached 155°F, 2–2½ hours.

4. Let the tenderloin rest under a foil tent for 15–20 minutes before slicing.

SWEET MOLASSES RIB TIPS

Ribs will never disappear as fast as these do. The molasses adds a full-bodied background sweetness, and it also helps the meat turn a gorgeous dark color. Cooking the ribs in a pan captures all the juice and braises the meat so it's juicy and fall-off-the-bone tender.

Prep time: 15 minutes   *Smoke time:* 3–4 hours   *Wood chips:* Hickory   *Serves:* 3–4

4 pounds rib tips

¼ cup blackstrap molasses

½ cup East Texas BBQ Rub (page 45)

2 jalapeños, quartered

1. Prepare the smoker's water pan according to the manufacturer's instructions and preheat the smoker to 230°F. While it heats, fill a medium bowl with water and add a couple handfuls of wood chips to soak.

2. Cut rib tips down into individual pieces and place in a 9 x 13-inch disposable foil pan (or two 8 x 8-inch pans), bone side up. Drizzle molasses over each rib tip and then rub over the whole rib to completely cover. Repeat process with the East Texas BBQ Rub, making sure each rib tip is covered completely. Toss jalapeño pieces into the pan(s).

3. Place pan(s) in the smoker and add a small handful of the soaked chips to the chip loading area. Adding more chips at least every 30 minutes, cook the rib tips until the internal temperature has reached 195°F, 3–4 hours. The meat will shrink on the bone and start to pull off.

Note: Try this recipe on a rack of baby back ribs. It's pure heaven! Skip the foil pans and just throw them on the smoker rack for 4–5 hours. Delish.

CAJUN-SPICED CHICKEN LEGS

These chicken legs have a little kick, but are so juicy and delicious that even the kids loved them. The best part is, even the skin gets a little crispy.

Prep time: 15 minutes   *Smoke time:* 2–2½ hours   *Wood chips:* Hickory   *Serves:* 6

6–7 pounds chicken legs (about 12 legs)

1 tablespoon coarse kosher salt

2½ teaspoons paprika

2 teaspoons garlic powder

1¼ teaspoons dried oregano

1¼ teaspoons dried thyme

1 teaspoon onion powder

1 teaspoon cayenne pepper

1 teaspoon coarsely ground black pepper

1. Prepare the smoker's water pan according to the manufacturer's instructions and preheat the smoker to 235°F. While it heats, fill a medium bowl with water and add 2 to 3 handfuls of wood chips to soak.

2. Remove the chicken pieces from packaging and pat dry. Combine salt, paprika, garlic powder, oregano, thyme, onion powder, cayenne pepper, and black pepper in a small bowl and rub each chicken leg with the seasonings until well coated.

3. Place chicken directly onto smoking rack. Add a small handful of the soaked wood chips to the chip loading area, and keep adding more chips at least every 30 minutes. The chicken is done when it reaches an internal temperature of 165°F, 2–2½ hours. Remove from the smoker and serve while hot.

Note: Not a spicy fan? Reduce the cayenne pepper to ½ teaspoon. However, if you can handle the heat, try adding a little more for a bigger spice kick!

BBQ BACON WRAPPED TENDERLOIN

Is there anything better than pork wrapped in more pork? Probably not! This is such a great recipe for a party—just make a lot more than you think you'll need because it goes fast. The bacon keeps the tenderloin extremely juicy. Serve with some fried okra or green beans for a fantastic supper.

Prep time: 30 minutes *Smoke time:* 2–3 hours *Wood chips:* Hickory *Serves:* 2–4

1 (1½–2-pound) pork tenderloin

½ tablespoon coarse kosher salt

1 teaspoon garlic powder

⅛–¼ cup East Texas BBQ Sauce (page 45)

6–8 slices thick-cut bacon

1. Prepare the smoker's water pan according to the manufacturer's instructions and preheat the smoker to 235°F. While it heats, fill a medium bowl with water and add a couple handfuls of wood chips to soak.

2. Dry the tenderloin with paper towels. Sprinkle salt and garlic powder all over the tenderloin and then rub with East Texas BBQ Sauce. Wrap the tenderloin with bacon strips, working from one end to the next. (Tip: Try to have the bacon ends start and stop on the underside of the tenderloin so they stay in place more easily while cooking.)

3. Place the tenderloin directly on the smoker rack and add a small handful of the soaked chips to the chip loading area. Adding more chips at least every 30 minutes, cook the tenderloin until the internal temperature has reached 155°F, 2–3 hours. Allow for more cooking time than a plain tenderloin to ensure the bacon is done.

4. Let the tenderloin rest under a foil tent for 15–20 minutes before slicing.

STICKY BBQ MOLASSES CHICKEN

Chicken breasts don't take long in the smoker at all, which makes them perfect for a weeknight meal. Adding molasses to the barbecue sauce is delicious.

Prep time: 10 minutes   *Smoke time:* 1–1½ hours   *Wood chips:* Hickory   *Serves:* 4

4 boneless skinless chicken breasts

½ teaspoon garlic powder

1 teaspoon coarse kosher salt

½ teaspoon coarsely ground black pepper

¼ cup East Texas BBQ Sauce (page 45)

¼ cup blackstrap molasses

1. Prepare the smoker's water pan according to the manufacturer's instructions and preheat the smoker to 275°F. While it heats, fill a medium bowl with water and add 3 or 4 handfuls of wood chips to soak.

2. Sprinkle the chicken breasts with garlic powder, salt, and pepper. In a small bowl, combine the barbecue sauce and molasses. Reserve half of the sauce for serving. Brush the chicken breasts lightly with the remaining sauce.

3. Set the chicken breasts on a middle rack of the smoker. Add a small handful of the soaked wood chips to the chip loading area, adding wood chips every 30 minutes. Baste chicken with additional sauce after 1 hour. The chicken is done when it reaches an internal temperature of 165°F, 1½–2 hours.

4. Serve while hot, along with reserved sauce, if desired.

SOUTH TEXAS-STYLE BARBECUE

South Texas–style barbecue is heavily influenced by neighboring Mexico and is not what you'd typically think of as barbecue in America. However, no Texas barbecue book would be complete with some delicious South Texas barbecue.

Barbacoa (Spanish for barbecue) is the star in the south, but it's almost an extinct type of barbecue in Texas. South-style barbecue uses mesquite wood with a lot of Mexican ingredients such as dried chiles, garlic, corn tortillas, cilantro, guacamole, and pico de gallo. Another star in South Texas–style barbecue is an ice-cold Big Red soda. There is even a Barbacoa and Big Red festival in Texas every year; the two go together perfectly.

BARBACOA

Traditional barbacoa is a whole cow head wrapped in banana leaves, then smoked underground. Sadly, this way of cooking barbacoa is almost extinct—there are only a few places left that cook it this way. Finding a cow head, or even just cow head meat, was hard to do, so I used a beef roast, which is an acceptable alternative if you can't get your hands on some head meat. If you can find head meat, definitely try it, as the flavor is out of this world.

Prep time: 15 minutes   *Smoke time:* 7–8 hours   *Wood chips:* Mesquite   *Serves:* 8–10

FOR THE BARBACOA

1 (3–4-pound) top round beef roast

1 head garlic (12–13 cloves), cloves separated and peeled

1 tablespoon coarse kosher salt

½ tablespoon coarsely ground black pepper

1 bay leaf

½ onion, cut into chunks

2 whole dried red chiles, stems discarded

½ cup beef stock

TO SERVE

warm corn tortillas

1 small white onion, finely diced (about 1 cup)

½ cup finely minced fresh cilantro leaves and tender stems

3–4 limes, cut into 8 wedges each

1. Prepare the smoker's water pan according to the manufacturer's instructions and preheat the smoker to 275°F. While it heats, fill a medium bowl with water and add 3 or 4 handfuls of wood chips to soak.

2. Place roast in an 8 x 8-inch disposable foil pan. Pierce the meat with 8–9 deep holes, and insert a clove of garlic in each hole, reserving the remaining garlic cloves. Rub the meat with salt and pepper. Add the bay leaf, onion, chilies, remaining garlic, and beef stock to the pan.

3. Place pan in the smoker and add a small handful of the soaked wood chips to the chip loading area. Adding more chips at least every 30 minutes, smoke for 7–8 hours, or until the internal temperature of the meat is 145°F–160°F and the meat shreds easily.

4. Remove roast from the pan and shred meat. Discard the bay leaf and add the cooking liquid, chiles, onion, and garlic to a blender and process until smooth. Pour over the shredded meat and stir to combine.

5. Mix the onion and cilantro. Serve the barbacoa with corn tortillas, fresh lime wedges, and onion/cilantro garnish.

SOUTH TEXAS SMOKED DUCK

Duck seems so exotic, but it's fairly common to make in Texas and in the South. Everyone loves to go duck hunting. It's also easy to find in the grocery store, usually near the frozen chicken and turkey, and occasionally found fresh at the meat counter. The mesquite wood adds a wonderful; however, the flavor of the duck varies depending on the type of duck you smoke. They are all delicious.

Prep time: 30 minutes *Smoke time:* 2–3 hours *Wood chips:* Mesquite *Serves:* 4

4–6 pound whole duck

2 teaspoons ground cumin

2 teaspoons coarse kosher salt

1 teaspoon ground coriander

1 teaspoon paprika

1 teaspoon chili powder

½ teaspoon garlic powder

½ teaspoon ground cinnamon

½ teaspoon coarsely ground black pepper

1. Prepare the smoker's water pan according to the manufacturer's instructions and preheat the smoker to 275°F. While it heats, fill a medium bowl with water and add 3 or 4 handfuls of wood chips to soak.

2. Remove duck from the packaging and remove any giblets and packets from the cavity of the duck. Rinse the bird and pat dry. Use a sharp knife and pierce the bird's skin and fat layer evenly all over. Go slowly and try not to pierce the meat, and stop when you feel the resistance of the meat. The fat is easy to penetrate.

3. In a small bowl, combine remaining ingredients and mix well. Rub all over the bird and inside the cavity. Place bird in the smoker, breast side up. Add a small handful of the soaked wood chips to the chip loading area, and keep adding more chips at least every 30 minutes. Smoke the duck for 2–3 hours, until the internal temperature reaches 165°F.

4. If the skin isn't crispy enough, heat a grill to high and grill for 1–2 minutes per side to crisp up the skin before serving.

Note: While a duck is larger than a chicken, their bones are bigger so there is less meat on a bird. The meat is all dark meat, even the breast. Due to the large amount of fat, do not skip piercing the skin and fat layer. It's essential to helping the fat drain out while cooking.

SMOKED MEXICAN BRISKET

Don't let the number of ingredients scare you! Throwing together this brisket is simple and requires very little hands-on time; the hardest part is remembering to start the marinade the night before. Slice up this brisket for street tacos and serve on top of corn tortillas with Pickled Red Onions, Avocado Cream (recipes follow), and fresh cilantro.

Prep time: 30 minutes, plus marinating overnight   *Smoke time:* 8–9 hours

Wood chips: Mesquite   *Serves:* 10–12

5–7 pound trimmed brisket

FOR THE MARINADE

2 cups orange juice

1½ cups soy sauce

juice of 6 limes

¼ cup extra virgin olive oil

3 tablespoons minced garlic

1 onion, roughly chopped

½ bunch cilantro, roughly chopped

1 tablespoon coarse kosher salt

FOR THE RUB

2 tablespoons chili powder

3 tablespoons ground cumin

2 tablespoons garlic powder

1 tablespoon onion powder

2 tablespoons coarse kosher salt

2 teaspoon cayenne pepper

1 teaspoon coarsely ground black pepper

1. Remove the brisket from its wrapping, dry with paper towels, and trim any remaining fat. In a 2½-gallon zip-top bag, add all the marinade ingredients, seal the bag, and squish to combine. Add the trimmed brisket to the bag and let it marinate overnight in the refrigerator, turning the bag every few hours so that all the meat gets covered with the marinade.

2. When ready to cook, prepare the smoker's water pan according to the manufacturer's instructions and preheat the smoker to 225°F. While it heats, fill a medium bowl with water and add 3 or 4 handfuls of wood chips to soak.

3. In a small bowl, combine the rub ingredients and stir to mix well. Remove brisket from the marinade and pat dry. Rub the dry rub mixture over the brisket, making sure to cover the brisket heavily.

4. Place the brisket in the smoker and add a small handful of the soaked wood chips to the chip loading area. Adding more chips at least every 30 minutes, smoke for 5–6 hours, or until the internal temperature of the meat is 165°F.

5. Remove the brisket from the smoker, wrap tightly in parchment paper, and return to smoker for another 3 hours. Do not add wood chips the last few hours, as no more smoke will penetrate the meat.

6. Remove from smoker and let rest in parchment paper for 30 minutes. Remove parchment paper and slice brisket into bite-size strips, removing any large pieces of fat.

PICKLED RED ONIONS

1 cup white vinegar

3 tablespoons granulated sugar

1½ tablespoons coarse kosher salt

½ teaspoon whole black peppercorns

1½ cups sliced red onion

In a medium saucepan over high heat, boil the vinegar, sugar, salt, and peppercorns until the sugar is completely dissolved, about 5 minutes. Add the sliced onions and continue boiling for 1–2 minutes. Remove from heat and let cool before transferring to a mason jar with a lid. Store in the refrigerator for 3–4 weeks.

AVOCADO CREAM

8 ounces sour cream

2 avocados

1 jalapeño pepper, roughly chopped

3 cloves garlic, finely minced

juice of 2 limes

½ teaspoon coarse kosher salt

Place all ingredients in a blender and process on high until smooth and creamy. Store in a mason jar with lid for 2–3 days. If the cream is too thick, thin with a little milk before using.

TEX-MEX BABY BACK RIBS

Ribs aren't necessarily a part of Southern Texas barbecue, but they should be. These tender baby backs are sweet with a hint of heat and Mexican oregano.

Prep time: 20 minutes   *Smoke time:* 5 hours   *Wood chips:* Mesquite   *Serves:* 3–4

⅓ cup brown sugar

3 tablespoons coarse kosher salt

1 tablespoon garlic powder

1 tablespoon onion powder

3 teaspoons ground cumin

3 teaspoons dried Mexican oregano

1 teaspoon coarsely ground black pepper

7–8 pounds (about 2 racks) baby back ribs

½ cup apple juice

1. Combine brown sugar, salt, garlic powder, onion powder, cumin, oregano, and black pepper in a small bowl and set aside. Prepare the ribs by removing the thin membrane from the back side (see page 31). Pat the ribs dry with a paper towel and liberally apply the prepared rub all over, including the ends and side pieces.

2. Prepare the smoker's water pan according to the manufacturer's instructions and preheat the smoker to 225°F. While it heats, fill a medium bowl with water and add 3 or 4 handfuls of wood chips to soak. Put the apple juice in a spray bottle.

3. Place ribs directly on the smoker racks, meat side facing up. Add a small handful of the soaked wood chips to the chip loading area, and keep adding more chips at least every 30 minutes. Spray the ribs heavily with apple juice every hour while the ribs are smoking. Smoke the ribs for about 5 hours, until the bones start to show and the meat is tender but not falling off the bone.

4. Let rest for 15 minutes under a foil tent and cut ribs apart to serve. No barbecue sauce needed.

CARNE ASADA

Using a combination of fresh lime and orange juices gives flank steak a wonderful citrus flavor. One of the best parts of carne asada is the crispy bits, so make sure to finish on the grill to get that crispy outside. Serve with corn tortillas, Pico de Gallo (recipe follows), and any other toppings you'd like, such as sour cream, avocado, and guacamole.

Prep time: 30 minutes, plus minimum 2 hours to marinate

Smoke time: 1½–2 hours, plus 5–6 minutes grill time   *Wood chips:* Mesquite   *Serves:* 6–8

2 pounds flank steak

¼ cup extra virgin olive oil

½ cup fresh lime juice (about 6 large limes)

½ cup fresh orange juice (about 2 oranges)

6 garlic cloves, peeled and smashed

2 tablespoons white vinegar

1 jalapeño, halved

½ cup roughly chopped cilantro

½ teaspoon coarse kosher salt

¼ teaspoon coarse ground black pepper

1. In a large zip-top bag, add all the ingredients, seal, and shake gently to combine. Let flank steak marinate for at least 2 hours in the refrigerator.

2. After meat has marinated, prepare the smoker's water pan according to the manufacturer's instructions and preheat the smoker to 275°F. While it heats, fill a medium bowl with water and add 3 or 4 handfuls of wood chips to soak.

3. Remove flank steak from the bag and place it on the smoker rack. Add a small handful of the soaked wood chips to the chip loading area, and keep adding more chips at least every 30 minutes. Smoke the flank steak for 1½–2 hours, until the internal temperature reaches 150°F. Heat a grill to high and cook flank steak for 2–3 minutes per side just to crisp up the meat.

PICO DE GALLO

2 cups diced onion, white or yellow (about ½–1 large onion)

2 cups diced plum tomato, juice and seeds removed (about 5–6)

1 cup chopped cilantro

2–3 jalapeños, seeded and deveined, finely diced

coarse kosher salt, to taste

juice of 1 lime (optional)

Combine the onion, tomato, cilantro, and jalapeño in a large bowl. Season with salt and lime juice as desired. Store in refrigerator for several hours or overnight to allow the flavors to develop.

Note: For a spicy pico, add in some seeds and veins.

AL PASTOR

Fresh pineapple and orange juice adds a sweetness to these classic Tex-Mex tacos. Serve with the simple toppings onion and cilantro plus a squeeze of fresh lime and some pineapple slices.

Prep time: 30 minutes, plus minimum 2 hours to marinate   *Smoke time:* 1½–2 hours

Wood chips: Mesquite   *Serves:* 3–4

½ large white onion, cut into chunks

1 pineapple, peeled, cored, and sliced

½ cup pineapple juice

½ cup fresh orange juice (about 2 oranges)

2 tablespoons chili powder

4 cloves garlic, smashed

2 tablespoons white vinegar

1 tablespoon coarse kosher salt

½ teaspoon Mexican oregano

3 pounds pork tenderloin

TO SERVE

warm corn tortillas

1 small white onion, finely diced

½ cup finely minced fresh cilantro leaves and tender stems

1 small pineapple, peeled, cored, and thinly sliced (optional)

3–4 limes, cut into 8 wedges each

1. Prepare the smoker's water pan according to the manufacturer's instructions and preheat the smoker to 275°F. While it heats, fill a medium bowl with water and add 3 or 4 handfuls of wood chips to soak.

2. In a heavy-duty blender, add onion, pineapple, pineapple juice, orange juice, chili powder, garlic, white vinegar, salt, and oregano. Blended until completely pureed and smooth. Add to a large zip-top bag.

3. Slice the tenderloin into 1-inch-thick slices and add to the zip-top bag. Seal the bag and refrigerate for at least 2 hours or up to overnight.

4. Remove tenderloin slices from the bag and place the tenderloin directly on the smoker rack. Add a small handful of the soaked chips to the chip loading area. Adding more chips at least every 30 minutes, cook the tenderloin until the internal temperature has reached 155°F, 1½–2 hours.

5. Chop slices into bite-size pieces and serve on corn tortillas with a mixture of the onion and cilantro, as well as the pineapple slices and a couple lime slices.

Note: If you can't find a ripe pineapple, use 1 can of pineapple chunks plus juice in place of the fresh pineapple and ½ cup juice.

CARNE GUISADA

Carne guisada is basically a thick Tex-Mex stew. It's thick and absolutely delicious when smoked with mesquite wood. Serve warm with rice or tortillas, avocado, and some fresh chopped cilantro for an easy supper.

Prep time: 30 minutes   *Smoke time:* 1½ hours   *Wood chips:* Mesquite   *Serves:* 6–8

3 pounds tri-tip, cut into 1-inch cubes

2 bell peppers, any variety, chopped

1 large white onion, chopped

2 cups beef broth

1 (15-ounce) can diced tomatoes

5 garlic cloves, finely minced

1 jalapeño, deveined, seeded, and finely diced

¼ cup flour

1 tablespoon ground cumin

1 tablespoon chili powder

1 teaspoon coarse kosher salt

½ teaspoon coarsely ground pepper

½ teaspoon Mexican oregano

½ teaspoon paprika

1. Prepare the smoker's water pan according to the manufacturer's instructions and preheat the smoker to 275°F. While it heats, fill a medium bowl with water and add 3 or 4 handfuls of wood chips to soak.

2. Place cubed meat in a 10-inch cast-iron pan (double check your pan fits the width of your smoker) and set the pan on a smoker rack. Add a small handful of the soaked wood chips to the chip loading area. After 30 minutes, gently stir the meat and add chopped bell peppers and onion to the pan, then add more wood chips.

3. Meanwhile, combine remaining ingredients in large bowl, and stir well to combine. After the meat and vegetables have smoked for 30 minutes, stir, then gently pour in the tomato mixture and stir to combine. Add one more handful of wood chips and cook for an additional 30 minutes.

4. Use a pot holder to remove cast-iron pan from smoker.

JALAPEÑO JERKY

Don't let the title fool you: It's not spicy, but it is full of amazing flavor. And there is no need for expensive store-bought jerky again—this will become your new favorite! Use a dark beer such as Negra Modelo for the best flavor.

Prep time: 40 minutes, plus 12 hours to marinate

Smoke time: 2–3 hours, plus 30 minutes cook time   *Wood chips:* Mesquite   *Serves:* Varies

2 cups dark Mexican beer

¼ cup fresh lime juice

¼ cup light brown sugar

2 tablespoons coarse kosher salt

2 tablespoons Worcestershire sauce

2 teaspoons coarsely ground black pepper

1½ teaspoons garlic powder

1 teaspoon onion powder

2–3 jalapeños, halved

2½–3 pounds eye of round roast, sliced about ⅛ inch thick

1. Combine all ingredients, except beef slices, in a medium saucepan over high heat. Bring to boil and cook for about 30 minutes, or until liquid is reduced by half, stirring occasionally. Place beef slices and marinade in a gallon-sized zip-top bag, seal, and refrigerate for 12 hours or overnight.

2. After marinating, prepare the smoker's water pan according to the manufacturer's instructions and preheat the smoker to 170°F or as low as your smoker goes. While it heats, fill a medium bowl with water and add 3 or 4 handfuls of wood chips to soak.

3. Remove meat from bag and pat dry with paper towels. Place meat in a single layer, without touching, on smoker racks. Add a small handful of the soaked wood chips to the chip loading area, and keep adding more chips at least every 30 minutes. Smoke the beef for 2–3 hours, until the meat is dried out. It should be able to bend and crack, but not break.

4. Jerky will last in a sealed container for 3–4 days on the counter or 1–2 weeks in the refrigerator.

Note: Ask your butcher to slice your roast as thin as possible for jerky.

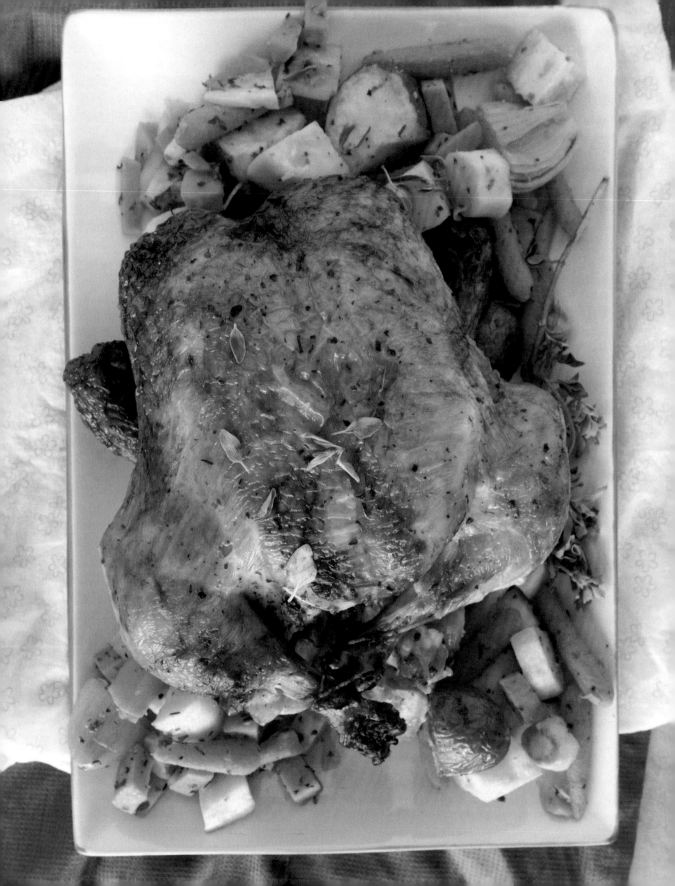

GARLIC AND OREGANO WHOLE CHICKEN

The ingredients seem simple, but they pack a ton of flavor. Smoke directly on the racks or use a vertical roaster for an impressive presentation. If you can't find Mexican oregano, regular dried oregano will work just fine.

Prep time: 15 minutes   *Smoke time:* 1½–2 hours   *Wood chips:* Mesquite   *Serves:* 4–6

2 tablespoons coarse kosher salt

2 tablespoons garlic powder

1 tablespoon ground cumin

1 tablespoon dried Mexican oregano

1 (4–6-pound) whole chicken

3 tablespoons canola or vegetable oil

1. Prepare the smoker's water pan according to the manufacturer's instructions and remove one or two of the top racks from smoker to make room for the standing chicken. Preheat the smoker to 275°F. While it heats, fill a medium bowl with water and add 3 or 4 handfuls of wood chips to soak.

2. Combine salt, garlic powder, cumin, and oregano in a small bowl; set aside. Remove the package of giblets from the cavity of the chicken, then rinse the bird and dry well. Rub the chicken with oil, and then coat it heavily with the seasoning mixture on both the inside and outside. Store any remaining mixture in an airtight container for up to 6 months.

3. Set the chicken on the vertical roaster and place it in the smoker, or place the chicken directly on the racks, breast side down. Add a small handful of the soaked wood chips to the chip loading area, and keep adding chips at least every 30 minutes. The chicken is done when it reaches an internal temperature of 165°F, about 1½–2 hours.

4. Let the chicken stand 10–15 minutes to cool before removing from the vertical roaster (or breast side down on the cutting board, if not using a vertical roaster) and carving.

Note: Got leftovers? This chicken makes a great chicken noodle soup! Pull any remaining chicken off the bone and add it to a large slow cooker along with a carton or two of chicken stock, a couple sliced carrots, a couple sliced celery stalks, 1 teaspoon coarse kosher salt, 1 teaspoon dried thyme, and ¼ teaspoon red pepper flakes, and cook on high all day. Add small pasta noodles 30 minutes before serving.

WEST TEXAS-STYLE BARBECUE

West Texas–style barbecue is more closely related to grilling than traditional smoking. It's done over direct heat with a mixture of hot coals and mesquite wood that has been reduced to hot ash. As the juice and fats from the meat drip down onto the mesquite wood ashes, it sends up smoke, which flavors the meat.

This style of barbecue was heavily influenced by the way cowboys prepared foods. There is not typically a sauce, and you'll find all sorts of meats from steak to prime rib to beef tenderloin. These meats are cooked hotter and faster, so they aren't necessarily as tender as East- or Central-style barbecue. Spicy pinto beans are the most common side dish served alongside West Texas barbecue.

WEST TEXAS BEEF RUB

Black pepper and garlic powder are the star of this rub. It's delicious on all cuts of beef with just a hint of heat and it's perfect whether smoking or grilling.

Prep time: 5 minutes   *Makes:* about ½ cup

3 tablespoons coarsely ground black pepper

2 tablespoons garlic powder

2 tablespoons coarse kosher salt

1 tablespoon onion powder

1½ teaspoons ground coriander

1½ teaspoons ground celery seed

¾ teaspoon cayenne pepper

1. Combine all the rub ingredients in an airtight container, stirring to mix well. Store in a cool, dark place for up to 6 months.

2. This recipe can be doubled or tripled and stored for up to 6 months for easy barbecue.

WEST TEXAS PORK AND CHICKEN RUB

This rub is a definite crowd-pleaser. It turns pork and chicken recipes into mouth-watering meals with a gorgeous, deep red color.

Prep time: 5 minutes   *Makes:* ½–¾ cup

3 tablespoons paprika

2 tablespoons garlic powder

2 tablespoons coarse kosher salt

1 tablespoon ground sage

1 tablespoon dried marjoram

1 tablespoon dried thyme

1. Combine all the rub ingredients in an airtight container, stirring to mix well. Store in a cool, dark place for up to 6 months.

2. This recipe can be doubled or tripled and stored for up to 6 months for easy barbecue.

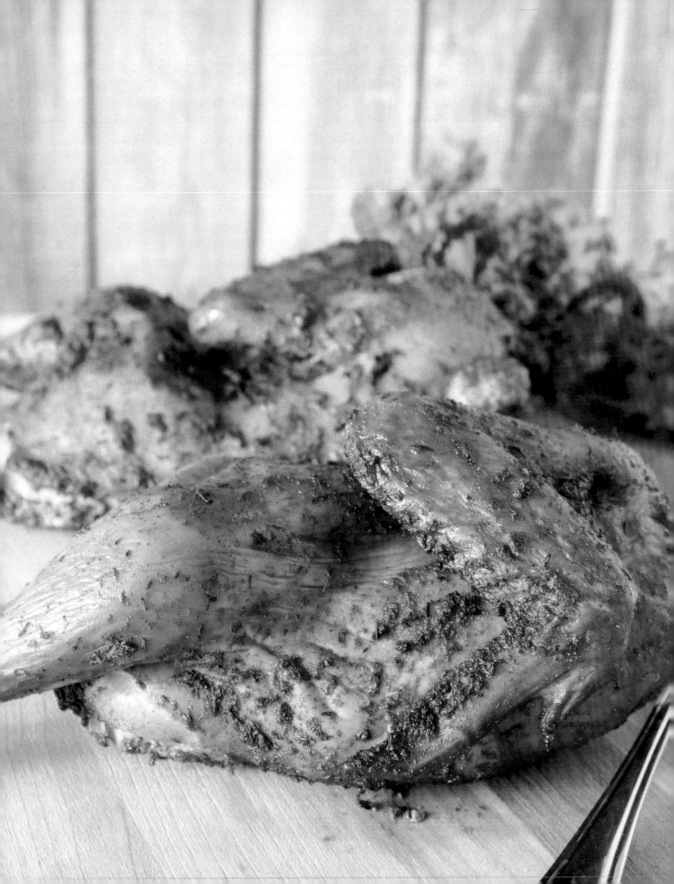

MESQUITE SMOKED HALF-CHICKENS

A moist, delicious chicken supper is only a few hours away. The mesquite wood adds a unique, amazing flavor to the chicken. If this is the only main dish being served, serve each person their own half-chicken. However, a whole chicken usually feeds 4–6. When picking up a whole chicken at the grocery store, ask the butcher to cut it in half. It doesn't cost any extra and makes the recipe prep much easier.

Prep time: 20 minutes, plus 1 hour to marinate   *Smoke time:* 1½–2 hours
Wood chips: Mesquite   *Serves:* 4–6

4½–5 pounds whole chicken, halved

2 tablespoons vegetable oil

4–5 tablespoons West Texas Pork and Chicken Rub (page 93)

1. To prepare the bird, remove any giblets and internal organs, then rinse and dry well. Place the chicken halves in a large zip-top bag. Rub with oil and then coat heavily with the seasoning on all sides. Seal and refrigerate for 1 hour.

2. Meanwhile, prepare the smoker's water pan according to the manufacturer's instructions. Preheat the smoker to 275°F. While it heats, fill a medium bowl with water and add 3 or 4 handfuls of mesquite wood chips to soak.

3. Set the chicken halves on a middle rack of the smoker, skin side up. Add a small handful of the soaked wood chips to the chip loading area and add chips again after about 30 minutes. Only use wood chips the first hour of cooking, as the mesquite flavor can overpower the chicken if too much is used. The chicken is done when it reaches an internal temperature of 165°F, 1½–2 hours.

4. Let stand 10–15 minutes to cool before carving.

PEPPERED BEEF TENDERLOIN

There really is nothing better than a beautiful piece of beef tenderloin. Mesquite wood adds a bold flavor to the beef that is truly delicious. Serving a whole beef tenderloin is perfect for a crowd, holiday, or dinner party. Serve with Spicy Pinto Beans (recipe follows).

Prep time: 20 minutes *Smoke time:* 3–3½ hours *Wood chips:* Mesquite *Serves:* 6–8

3½–4 pounds whole beef tenderloin

2–3 tablespoons West Texas Beef Rub
(page 93)

1. Prepare the smoker's water pan according to the manufacturer's instructions. Preheat the smoker to 275°F. While it heats, fill a medium bowl with water and add 3 or 4 handfuls of mesquite wood chips to soak.

2. Remove tenderloin from packaging, rinse, and pat dry. Remove any silver skin and large pieces of fat; a little fat is okay and desired for a moist tenderloin. Liberally cover the tenderloin with West Texas Beef Rub and massage it gently into the meat.

3. Add the meat to the prepared smoker and smoke for 3–3½ hours, adding wood chips every 30 minutes for the first 2 hours. Continue smoking until desired doneness is reached, or until at least 150–155°F for medium-rare.

4. Let stand 10–15 minutes to cool before carving.

Note: Use the best coarsely ground black pepper you can find (or crack your own) as the flavor of the pepper really stands out.

SPICY PINTO BEANS

3 (15-ounce) cans pinto beans or 6 cups cooked pinto beans

1 tablespoon coarse kosher salt

2 teaspoons coarsely ground black pepper

½ large white onion, finely diced

1 jalapeño, finely diced

Place all ingredients in a slow cooker on low for 3–4 hours. Stir occasionally.

PERFECT WEEKNIGHT PORK CHOPS

Smoking doesn't have to be an all-day event. The right cut of meat can be done in under an hour and makes a great weeknight supper.

Prep time: 5 minutes   *Smoke time:* 45–60 minutes   *Wood chips:* Mesquite   *Serves:* 4

4 bone-in pork chops

1–1½ tablespoons West Texas Pork and Chicken Rub (page 93)

1. Prepare the smoker's water pan according to the manufacturer's instructions. Preheat the smoker to 275°F. While it heats, fill a medium bowl with water and add a handful of mesquite wood chips to soak.

2. Sprinkle the rub on both sides of the pork chops and place them in the smoker. Add wood chips at the beginning of the cooking time only.

3. Check the pork chops for doneness after smoking for 45 minutes. Pork will dry out quickly and shouldn't be overcooked. Cooking time will depend on how thick the pork chops are.

RED-EYE BRISKET

West Texas–style barbecue is cowboy barbecue, and cowboys love their coffee to stay awake on the range. This recipe is a great way to use up leftover coffee grounds if you have them; plus, it's downright delectable. Due to the high temperature and fast cooking time for West Texas barbecue, this brisket won't be as moist, but it's still delicious.

Prep time: 20 minutes   *Smoke time:* 6–7 hours   *Wood chips:* Mesquite   *Serves:* 10–12

5–6 pounds trimmed brisket

½ cup ground coffee or used coffee grounds

2 tablespoons coarse kosher salt

2 tablespoons brown sugar

2 teaspoons smoked paprika

1 tablespoon chili powder

1 teaspoon onion powder

1 teaspoon ground cumin

½ teaspoon coarsely ground black pepper

1. Prepare the smoker's water pan according to the manufacturer's instructions and preheat the smoker to 275°F. While it heats, fill a medium bowl with water and add 3 or 4 handfuls of wood chips to soak.

2. Remove the brisket from its wrapping, dry with paper towels, and trim any remaining fat. In a small bowl, combine coffee grounds, salt, brown sugar, paprika, chili powder, onion powder, cumin, and pepper. Rub the mixture over the brisket, making sure to cover it heavily.

3. Place the brisket in the smoker and add a small handful of the soaked wood chips to the chip loading area. Adding more chips at least every 30 minutes, smoke for 4 hours, or until the internal temperature of the meat is 165°F.

4. Remove the brisket from the smoker, wrap tightly in parchment paper, and return to smoker for another 2–3 hours. Do not add wood chips the last few hours, as no more smoke will penetrate the meat.

5. Remove the brisket from the smoker and let rest, in the parchment paper, for 30 minutes. Remove parchment paper and slice brisket for serving. Serve on a platter or on buns as a sandwich.

ROASTED GARLIC RIBS

These sweet roasted garlic ribs are a garlic lover's dream come true. The garlic really mellows out and adds such a divine flavor to these smoked babies. Both East Texas BBQ Sauce (page 45) or Simple Texas BBQ Sauce (page 21) go well with these ribs.

Prep time: 10 minutes, plus 1 hour to marinate   *Smoke time:* 5 hours   *Wood chips:* Mesquite

Serves: 3–4

7–8 pounds (about 2 racks) baby back ribs

FOR THE RUB

½ cup garlic powder

½ cup brown sugar

1 tablespoon coarse kosher salt

FOR BASTING SAUCE

2 heads roasted garlic

¼ cup brown sugar

¼ cup soy sauce

2 tablespoons vegetable or chicken broth

1 teaspoon Worcestershire sauce

pinch of coarse kosher salt

TO SERVE

1 cup barbecue sauce (optional)

1. Combine the garlic powder, brown sugar, and salt in a small bowl and set aside. Prepare the ribs by removing the thin membrane from the back side (see page 31). Pat the ribs dry with a paper towel and liberally apply the prepared rub all over, including the ends and side pieces. Place the ribs in a large zip-top bag and refrigerate for 1 hour.

2. Prepare the smoker's water pan according to the manufacturer's instructions and preheat the smoker to 275°F. While it heats, fill a medium bowl with water and add 3 or 4 handfuls of wood chips to soak.

3. Use tongs to remove the ribs from the bag and place them directly on the smoker racks, meat side facing up. Add a small handful of the soaked wood chips to the chip loading area, and keep adding more chips at least every 30 minutes.

4. While the ribs start to smoke, combine all the ingredients for the basting sauce in a medium saucepan over medium-high heat. Simmer for 10 minutes, stirring occasionally. Pour sauce in a blender or use an immersion blender to completely puree. Baste the ribs every 30 minutes with sauce.

5. Smoke the ribs for 4–5 hours, until the bones start to show and the meat is tender but not falling off the bone.

6. Let rest for 15 minutes under a foil tent, cut ribs apart to serve, and serve with barbecue sauce, if desired.

Note: I buy pre-roasted garlic at my local grocery store's olive bar. If you can't find pre-roasted garlic, slice the top off garlic bulb (exposing each clove) and drizzle a few teaspoons of olive oil over the exposed garlic cloves. Cover the bulb with aluminum foil. Bake at 400°F for 30–35 minutes or until a knife is easily inserted and the cloves feel soft when pressed.

SWEET AND TANGY PORK SHOULDER

This pork shoulder is so tender and juicy and full of mesquite flavor, this will be your go-to pulled pork for sandwiches from now on!

Prep time: 30 minutes   *Smoke time:* 10–12 hours   *Wood chips:* Mesquite   *Serves:* 20

7 pounds pork butt (shoulder)

⅓ cup brown sugar

3 tablespoons coarse kosher salt

1 tablespoon garlic powder

1 tablespoon onion powder

¼ cup prepared yellow mustard

½–1 cup apple juice

1. Prepare the smoker's water pan according to the manufacturer's instructions and preheat the smoker to 230°F. While it heats, fill a medium bowl with water and add 3 or 4 handfuls of wood chips to soak.

2. Remove the pork butt from packaging and trim off any large pieces of fat. Pat dry and set aside. Combine brown sugar, salt, garlic powder, and onion powder in a small bowl. Rub pork with yellow mustard, then apply rub liberally to prepared pork butt.

3. Place the pork butt in the smoker and add a small handful of the soaked wood chips to the chip loading area. Add more chips at least every 30 minutes. Meanwhile, pour apple juice into a spray bottle. Spray pork heavily every hour with the apple juice.

4. After 6 hours of smoking, remove pork from smoker, wrap in heavy-duty foil, and return to smoker for an additional 4–6 hours. Do not add any more wood chips after the pork is wrapped. The pork is done when it shreds easily with two forks.

5. Remove from smoker and let pork rest in the foil 10–20 minutes before shredding.

WEST TEXAS DRY BABY BACK RIBS

Using apple juice in a spray bottle keeps these ribs moist while adding a delicious sweet flavor. Just make sure to use a good-quality 100 percent apple juice.

Prep time: 20 minutes   *Smoke time:* 5 hours   *Wood chips:* Mesquite   *Serves:* 3–4

⅓ cup brown sugar

3 tablespoons coarse kosher salt

1 tablespoon garlic powder

1 tablespoon onion powder

1 teaspoon coarsely ground black pepper

7–8 pounds (about 2 racks) baby back ribs

½ cup apple juice

1. Combine brown sugar, salt, garlic powder, onion powder, and black pepper in a small bowl and set aside. Prepare the ribs by removing the thin membrane from the back side (see page 31). Pat the ribs dry with a paper towel and liberally apply the prepared rub all over, including the ends and side pieces.

2. Prepare the smoker's water pan according to the manufacturer's instructions and preheat the smoker to 225°F. While it heats, fill a medium bowl with water and add 3 or 4 handfuls of wood chips to soak. Meanwhile, put the apple juice in a spray bottle.

3. Place ribs directly on the smoker racks, meat side facing up. Add a small handful of the soaked wood chips to the chip loading area, and keep adding more chips at least every 30 minutes. Spray the ribs heavily with apple juice every hour while the ribs are smoking. Smoke the ribs for about 5 hours, until the bones start to show and the meat is tender but not falling off the bone.

4. Let rest for 15 minutes under a foil tent, then cut ribs apart to serve. No need for barbecue sauce!

WEST TEXAS MESQUITE RIBEYE STEAKS

A delicious steak dinner is just a few hours away. Cooking them in the smoker is an easy way to cook on a busy weekend. These steaks cook perfectly without a lot of fuss or attention. Once you've had mesquite steaks, you might not ever want them any other way!

Prep time: 10 minutes   *Smoke time:* 1¼–2 hours   *Wood chips:* Mesquite   *Serves:* 4

2 teaspoons coarsely ground black pepper

2 teaspoons coarse kosher salt

1 teaspoon cayenne pepper

1 teaspoon chili powder

1 teaspoon garlic powder

4 (6-ounce) ribeye steaks

1. In a small bowl, combine the black pepper, salt, cayenne pepper, chili powder, and garlic powder. Sprinkle 1 to 2 teaspoons of this rub mixture on all sides of each steak. Store any leftover seasoning in an airtight container for up to 6 months.

2. Prepare the smoker's water pan according to the manufacturer's instructions and preheat the smoker to 275°F. While it heats, fill a medium bowl with water and add 1 or 2 handfuls of wood chips to soak.

3. Place steaks directly on a smoker rack. Add a small handful of the soaked wood chips to the chip loading area. Add more wood chips every 30 minutes. Smoke the steaks for 1¼–2 hours, or until they are done the way you like them. For a medium steak, cook to an internal temperature of 155°F.

Note: Sirloin steaks cooked this way are delicious too.

GARLIC PEPPER PRIME RIB

Don't wait for the holidays to smoke this prime rib! It's perfectly flavored, has a thick crust, and is so juicy that you'll need an extra napkin. Use a disposable foil pan placed under the prime rib while smoking to catch any drippings, which you can use to make Au Jus (recipe follows). Serve with horseradish sauce or Au Jus, if desired.

Prep time: 10 minutes   *Smoke time:* 1½–2½   *Wood chips:* Mesquite   *Serves:* 6–8

¼ cup minced garlic (about 20 cloves)

2 tablespoons coarse kosher salt

1¼ tablespoons coarsely ground black pepper

1 tablespoon brown sugar

1 teaspoon dried thyme

1 (7–8-pound) bone-in beef prime rib roast

1. Prepare the smoker's water pan according to the manufacturer's instructions and preheat the electric smoker to 275°F. While it heats, fill a medium bowl with water and add 3 or 4 handfuls of wood chips to soak.

2. Combine garlic, salt, pepper, brown sugar, and thyme in a small bowl. Rub the mixture on the top of the prime rib. It will be very thick (you'll use all the rub). This will add a delicious crust to the outside of your prime rib.

3. When the smoker is ready, place the prime rib directly on a smoker rack, and add a small handful of the soaked wood chips to the chip loading area. Keep adding chips at least every 30 minutes. Use a meat thermometer to monitor the temperature of the roast, and remove it from the smoker when it is about 10°F under the recommended temperature for the degree of doneness you want. Prime rib takes anywhere from 1½–2½ hours, depending on whether you like yours rare, medium-rare, or medium.

4. When the meat is close to being ready, take it out of the smoker and let the meat rest for 15–20 minutes under a loose foil tent to finish cooking and allow the juices to be absorbed back into the meat.

5. Cut and serve in ½-inch-thick slices.

Temperature Guide

Using a meat thermometer ensures you stop cooking at the perfect temperature. Remove the prime rib from the smoker 10°F before it reaches the recommended temperature for the degree of doneness.

Rare prime rib is done at 125°F–130°F.

Medium-rare prime rib is done at 135°F.

Medium prime rib is done at 140°F.

AU JUS

drippings from prime rib

3 cups beef stock or broth

1 teaspoon soy sauce

⅛ teaspoon garlic powder

salt and pepper, to taste

Place the drippings and stock or broth in a medium saucepan, skim off any fat, and bring to a boil over medium-high heat. Reduce heat to low; whisk in soy sauce, garlic powder, and salt and pepper, to taste.

CHILI PIE

Take this classic chili dish and smoke it up! The mesquite wood gives it such a deep, smoky flavor. Top it with loads of cheese, onions, and, of course, Frito chips for a delicious supper.

Prep time: 15 minutes   *Smoke time:* 2 hours, plus 20 minutes cook time

Wood chips: Mesquite   *Serves:* 4–6

1 ½ pounds lean ground beef

1 (15-ounce) can pinto beans, drained and rinsed

1 (15-ounce) can tomato sauce

2 cups water

1 tablespoon all-purpose or gluten-free flour

1 tablespoon chili powder

2 tablespoons dried minced onion

1 teaspoon coarse kosher salt

1 teaspoon dried minced garlic

1 teaspoon ground cumin

½ teaspoon red pepper flakes

½ teaspoon sugar

TO SERVE

1 cup diced onion

1 cup shredded cheddar cheese

1 bag Fritos or corn chips

1. Prepare the smoker's water pan according to the manufacturer's instructions and preheat the electric smoker to 275°F. While it heats, fill a medium bowl with water and add 3 or 4 handfuls of mesquite chips to soak.

2. Meanwhile, cook the ground beef in a large cast-iron pot on the stovetop over high heat. Stir and break the meat apart until it is crumbly and no longer pink. Drain off any fat liquid and add the beans, tomato sauce, water, and remaining ingredients. Stir well to combine.

3. Place pot on the top rack of the smoker. Add a small handful of the soaked wood chips to the chip loading area. Stir the chili and add more chips at least every 30 minutes. The chili is already fully cooked, but let it smoke for about 2 hours to let the flavors fully develop.

4. To serve, ladle the chili into bowls and top with chopped onions, cheese, and a handful of Fritos.

Note: If your cast iron pot has feet, then it won't work on a flat-top stove. Use a separate stockpot to cook the chili mixture and then transfer to the cast iron pot before placing in smoker.

SPICY COWBOY CHICKEN WINGS

These wings are crispy and spicy, and you might not want to share. They are always a hit and since they are so easy, they are the perfect addition to any party!

Prep time: 15 minutes, plus 30 minutes to marinate   *Smoke time:* 1½ hours

Wood chips: Mesquite   *Serves:* 2–3

3 pounds chicken wing pieces (thawed, if frozen)

½ cup hot wing sauce, like Frank's Red Hot Sauce

¼ cup West Texas Pork and Chicken Rub (page 93)

¼ teaspoon cayenne pepper

ranch dressing and fresh vegetables, for serving

1. Prepare the smoker's water pan according to the manufacturer's instructions and preheat the smoker to 275°F. While it heats, fill a medium bowl with water and add a couple handfuls of wood chips to soak.

2. Using paper towels, pat each chicken wing dry (this helps the skin crisp). Place the wings in a large zip-top bag, add the hot sauce, and seal. Shake the wings around in the bag to completely coat them with the hot sauce and then let them sit for 30 minutes in the refrigerator.

3. Combine the rub and cayenne pepper in a small bowl, stirring to mix well. Add to the bag with the chicken wings, reseal, and move the chicken pieces around in the bag to thickly coat them with the seasoning mixture.

4. Remove the chicken wings from the bag and carefully place them in a single layer directly on the smoker racks. Add a small handful of the soaked chips to the chip loading area, and keep adding more chips at least every 30 minutes. The chicken is done when it reaches an internal temperature of 165°F, about 1½ hours.

5. Serve the wings hot along with ranch dressing and fresh vegetables.

COFFEE RUBBED TRI-TIP

This tri-tip is delicious for breakfast or dinner with its shot of coffee flavor. It's best served medium-rare to medium and sliced very thin. Serve with Spicy Pinto Beans (page 97) or with four tortillas and your favorite salsa.

Prep time: 10 minutes   *Smoke time:* 2–3 hours   *Wood chips:* Mesquite   *Serves:* 5–6

3 tablespoons ground coffee or instant coffee granules

2 tablespoons West Texas Beef Rub (page 93)

1 teaspoon dried rosemary

2½–3 pounds tri-tip

1 tablespoon extra virgin olive oil

1. Prepare the smoker's water pan according to the manufacturer's instructions. Preheat the smoker to 225°F. While it heats, fill a medium bowl with water and add 3 or 4 handfuls of wood chips to soak.

2. In a small bowl, combine ground coffee, West Texas Beef Rub, and rosemary.

3. Remove the tri-tip from its packaging, rinse, and pat dry. Rub olive oil all over the tri-tip and then liberally rub with spices.

4. Place the meat in the smoker and add a small handful of the soaked wood chips to the chip loading area. Adding more chips every 30 minutes, smoke for 2–3 hours. Continue smoking until desired doneness is reached or until it reaches at least 150–155°F for a medium-rare to medium tri-tip.

5. Let stand under a foil tent for 10–15 minutes to cool before carving.

DESSERTS

No Texas barbecue is complete without a delicious dessert or two. And growing up in Texas, we always had a few sweet staples. My mom and Granny passed down their treasured recipes to me, so these are the real deal. I've tweaked them only slightly over the years.

I've included my favorite desserts for the perfect ending to your barbecue supper. Most aren't smoked, because they just aren't done that way in the Lone Star State. However, there are occasional smoked ingredients, if you want to try them. My all-time favorite dessert is pecan pie, so you'll find it in this chapter for a fun smoky twist on an old classic.

SMOKED PECAN PIE

Pecan pie is a traditional Texas holiday dessert, but it's great all year long. Use pecan wood in the smoker for an unbelievable twist on this classic dessert.

Prep time: 30 minutes   *Smoke time:* 2½–3 hours   *Wood chips:* Pecan   *Serves:* 6

1 unbaked Homemade Pie Dough (recipe follows) or store-bought dough

3 eggs

½ cup sugar

1 cup light corn syrup

2 tablespoons butter, melted

1 teaspoon vanilla extract

8 ounces (about 1 cup) pecan halves or pieces

1. Roll out the pie dough and place it in a deep pie pan (a regular pie pan will not hold all the filling).

2. In a large bowl, beat the eggs well and then add sugar, corn syrup, and vanilla. Slowly add in melted butter and mix well.

3. Place the pecans in the bottom of the pie pan. Gently pour the egg mixture over the pecans; they will float to the top. Use a spoon to gently arrange the pecans in an even layer.

4. Smoke for 2½–3 hours, until crust is golden brown and filling is mostly set. Pie may appear soft in the middle, but it should firm up when cool.

In the oven: Place pie in a 420°F oven for 10 minutes, and then turn down the heat to 300°F and continue baking for 30–40 minutes, until crust is golden brown and filling is mostly set.

HOMEMADE PIE DOUGH

Prep time: 10 minutes, plus 30 minutes to chill   *Makes:* 2 crusts

2½ cups all-purpose flour

2 tablespoons sugar

½ teaspoon salt

1 cup (2 sticks) cold, unsalted butter, cut into small pieces

6 tablespoons very cold water

1. Combine flour, sugar, and salt in the bowl of a food processor. Process briefly to blend dry ingredients. Add the butter and pulse 8–10 times in 1-second pulses to work the butter into the flour. Stop when the mixture is pea sized.

2. Pour the water into the mixture and do short pulses to incorporate water. The dough should be just wet enough that it will stick together when pinched. Add additional water by the tablespoon, as needed.

3. Divide the dough in half and shape each half into a ball, wrap each in plastic wrap, and chill in the refrigerator for at least 30 minutes.

4. Remove from the refrigerator. Roll out the dough on a lightly floured work surface. Use as directed in your desired pie recipe.

BANANA PUDDING

A summer staple, banana pudding is a classic vanilla pudding with the addition of fresh, ripe bananas and lots of vanilla cookies. This cool, light dessert is perfect for the barbecue season.

Prep time: 20 minutes   *Cook time:* 10–15 minutes   *Chill time:* 1 hour   *Serves:* 4

¼ cup cornstarch

½ cup sugar

¼ teaspoon salt

2 cups milk

½ teaspoon vanilla extract

½ (11-ounce) box vanilla wafer cookies

3 bananas, peeled and thinly sliced

whipped cream, for serving

1. Place cornstarch, sugar, and salt in a medium saucepan and gently whisk until combined. Add milk very slowly while stirring constantly. Cook over medium heat and continue stirring slowly and constantly until the mixture thickens and starts to boil, 10–15 minutes. Let the pudding boil for 30–45 seconds while stirring. Remove the pan from heat and stir in the vanilla.

2. Place a single layer of cookies in the bottom of 4 dessert cups, then pour ⅛ of the pudding into each cup. Add a layer of sliced bananas, more cookies, and top with remaining pudding. Add more cookies on top and refrigerate for at least 1 hour.

3. Serve with a dollop of whipped cream.

TEXAS SHEET CAKE

Texas sheet cake is rich, moist, super chocolatey, and also super easy to make. Don't skip the cinnamon— that's what makes this cake! The frosting is traditionally made with pecans; try adding in some smoked pecans for a fun change (or leave the nuts out if you prefer).

Prep time: 30 minutes   *Cook time:* 20 minutes   *Serves:* 20

CAKE

2 cups all-purpose flour

2 cups sugar

¼ cup cocoa powder

1 cup water

1 cup (2 sticks) butter

1 teaspoon baking soda

½ cup sour cream

2 eggs, lightly beaten

1 teaspoon vanilla extract

1 teaspoon ground cinnamon

FROSTING

½ cup (1 stick) butter

3½ tablespoons cocoa powder

⅓ cup milk

1 pound powdered sugar, sifted

1 teaspoon vanilla extract

⅔ cup smoked pecans (page 123) (optional)

1. Preheat the oven to 400°F and spray a 16 x 11 x 1-inch sheet pan with nonstick cooking spray. Set aside.

2. Combine the flour and sugar in a large mixing bowl. Combine the cocoa, water, and butter in a saucepan and bring to a rapid boil over high heat. Pour the cocoa mixture over the flour/

sugar and, using an electric mixer, beat on a medium-low speed until well combined. Add the sour cream, eggs, vanilla, and cinnamon and continue mixing on a medium-low speed until everything is mixed well.

3. Pour the batter into the prepared sheet pan and bake for 20 minutes or until a toothpick inserted into the middle comes out clean. Let cool for 10–15 minutes while preparing the frosting.

4. To prepare the frosting, combine the butter, cocoa powder, and milk in a medium-sized saucepan. Heat over medium heat until it boils, about 5 minutes. Move mixture to a bowl for if using an electric mixer or a glass bowl if using a handheld mixer. Add remaining ingredients, except pecans, and beat on medium speed until well combined. Stir in pecans, if desired, then pour over warm cake. Use a butter knife or off set spatula to spread frosting over cake.

Note: Cake can be made in a 9 x 13-inch pan, if desired. Increase cooking time to 35–40 minutes.

SMOKED NUTS

Smoked nuts are great for adding to brownies, cheese platters, sauces, and just general snacking.

Prep time: 5 minutes   *Cook time:* 1–1½ hours   *Wood chips:* Maple   *Makes:* 2–3 cups

2 to 3 cups raw, shelled nuts (walnuts, pecans, cashews, or other nuts of your choice)

1. Preheat the smoker to 210°F without using the water pan. While it heats, fill a medium bowl with water and add 3 or 4 handfuls of maple wood chips to soak.

2. Spread the nuts in a disposable 9 x 13-inch foil pan and set the pan in the smoker. Add a small handful of the soaked maple chips to the chip loading area, and keep adding more chips at least every 30 minutes. Stir the nuts every 30 minutes until all the nuts are smoked, 1–1½ hours.

3. Remove the pan from the smoker and let the nuts cool to room temperature before serving or using them in a recipe. You can store the smoked nuts in an airtight container for up to 3 weeks.

Tip: This same technique works to smoke rolled oats for cookies or oatmeal, coconut flakes for cookies and cakes, and even flour for cakes and breads.

BREAD PUDDING WITH BOURBON SAUCE

The bread pudding is delicious, but adding the bourbon sauce really takes it to another level. It's a great and easy way to feed dessert to a crowd of barbecue lovers. It's perfect served at room temperature or slightly warmed. However, plan ahead: The bread needs some time to sit on the counter to dry out before you can add the other ingredients.

Prep time: 30 minutes   *Cook time:* 1 hour   *Serves:* 12

BREAD PUDDING

1 loaf French bread (about 16 ounces)

4 cups milk

3 large eggs, beaten

2 cups granulated sugar

3 tablespoons butter, melted

2 tablespoons vanilla extract

1 cup raisins

1 cup smoked nuts (page 123) (optional)

BOURBON SAUCE

½ cup (1 stick) butter

½ cup granulated sugar

½ cup firmly packed brown sugar

½ cup heavy whipping cream

1 tablespoon vanilla extract

2 tablespoons bourbon

1. Cut the French bread loaf into 1-inch cubes and let sit out for 2 hours to overnight to dry out.

2. Preheat the oven to 325°F and spray a 9 x 13-inch baking pan with nonstick cooking spray.

3. In a large bowl, combine milk, eggs, sugar, butter, and vanilla. Stir well to combine, then gently mix in raisins and nuts. Add the bread cubes and stir well. Pour bread mixture into the prepared pan.

4. Bake uncovered for 1 hour, or until firm. Cool in the pan at least 20 minutes before serving.

5. While the bread pudding bakes, prepare the bourbon sauce by combining the butter, granulated sugar, brown sugar, and whipping cream in a small saucepan. Cook over medium heat, stirring occasionally, for 5–8 minutes or until mixture thickens and comes to a full boil. Remove from heat and stir in vanilla and bourbon carefully. Let the sauce cool to room temperature before serving.

6. Spoon warm pudding into individual dessert dishes; serve with bourbon sauce.

PEACH AND BLUEBERRY COBBLER

My family always made peach cobbler growing up. It was my sister's specialty. My version includes blueberries, which adds a lovely flavor to the cobbler.

Prep time: 20 minutes   *Cook time:* 45–60 minutes   *Serves:* 10

8 cups frozen sliced peaches or about 2 (16-ounce) bags

1 cup fresh blueberries (about 1 pint)

½ cup all-purpose flour

1½ cups granulated sugar, plus more for sprinkling

½ cup (1 stick) butter

½ cup water

1 unbaked Homemade Pie Dough (page 120) or store-bought dough

1. Preheat the oven to 400°F and spray a 9 x 13-inch baking pan with nonstick cooking spray.

2. Place the fruit in the pan. In a small bowl, combine flour and sugar then pour evenly over fruit. Dot with butter and pour water over the pan.

3. Roll out pie dough. Slice into long, thin slices and place them over the fruit in a lattice design. Sprinkle the dough with a little extra sugar. Bake for 45–60 minutes or until it's hot and bubbly, and the pie dough is lightly browned.

DECADENT BROWNIES WITH SMOKED PECANS

Making brownies from scratch is so easy, and the results are so much better than a boxed mix. These fudgy brownies are always a crowd pleaser.

Prep time: 30 minutes   *Cook time:* 35–40 minutes   *Serves:* 12

⅔ cup coconut oil

1 ¼ cups sugar

¼ cup water

4 cups (24 ounces) semisweet chocolate chips, divided

2 teaspoons vanilla extract

4 eggs

1 ½ cups all-purpose flour

½ teaspoon baking soda

½ teaspoon salt

1 cup smoked nuts (page 123)

1. Preheat the oven to 325°F. Spray a 9 x 13-inch baking pan with nonstick cooking spray.

2. In a heavy saucepan, bring the coconut oil, sugar, and water to a boil, stirring constantly over medium-high heat until the sugar is dissolved, 2–3 minutes.

3. Remove from the heat and stir in 2 cups of chocolate chips until melted. Let cool slightly, then stir in the vanilla.

4. In a large bowl, whisk the eggs and gradually add the chocolate mixture, stirring with a wooden spoon until completely mixed.

5. In a medium bowl, mix together the flour, baking soda, and salt. Add the flour mixture to the chocolate mixture and mix well to combine. Stir in the remaining chocolate chips and smoked nuts.

6. Spread the batter into the prepared baking pan. Bake for 35–40 minutes or until a toothpick inserted into the middle comes out clean.

7. Serve warm or at room temperature.

CONVERSION CHARTS

Volume Conversions

U.S.	U.S. Equivalent	Metric
1 tablespoon (3 teaspoons)	½ fluid ounce	15 milliliters
¼ cup	2 fluid ounces	60 milliliters
⅓ cup	3 fluid ounces	90 milliliters
½ cup	4 fluid ounces	120 milliliters
⅔ cup	5 fluid ounces	150 milliliters
¾ cup	6 fluid ounces	180 milliliters
1 cup	8 fluid ounces	240 milliliters
2 cups	16 fluid ounces	480 milliliters

Weight Conversions

U.S.	Metric
½ ounce	15 grams
1 ounce	30 grams
2 ounces	60 grams
¼ pound	115 grams
⅓ pound	150 grams
½ pound	225 grams
¾ pound	350 grams
1 pound	450 grams

Temperature Conversions

Fahrenheit (°F)	Celsius (°C)	Fahrenheit (°F)	Celsius (°C)
70°F	20°C	220°F	105°C
100°F	40°C	240°F	115°C
120°F	50°C	260°F	125°C
130°F	55°C	280°F	140°C
140°F	60°C	300°F	150°C
150°F	65°C	325°F	165°C
160°F	70°C	350°F	175°C
170°F	75°C	375°F	190°C
180°F	80°C	400°F	200°C
190°F	90°C	425°F	220°C
200°F	95°C	450°F	230°C

ABOUT THE AUTHOR

Wendy O'Neal is the creator of the popular food and homemaking blog *Around My Family Table* and the author of *Smoke It Like a Pit Master in Your Electric Smoker*. Her passion for sharing recipes and tips to help families gather around the supper table inspired her to begin the site in 2009. Wendy's award-winning recipes have been featured on numerous online sites, including the Huffington Post, BuzzFeed, FoxNews.com, MSN.com, Today.com, eHow, Epicurious, and many more. Wendy has also competed at the World Food Championships in the Food Blogger Division.

Wendy's mom taught her to cook at an early age, but it wasn't until college and marriage to her high school sweetheart that she really found her love of cooking and developed her culinary skills. She taught herself how to grill and smoke shortly after she married, and since then she and her husband have had something going in the smoker almost every weekend.

Wendy, her husband, and their two children live in Phoenix, Arizona. You can find Wendy at AroundMyFamilyTable.com, sharing her latest recipes, cooking tips, and homemaking ideas to help *your* family come together at the supper table.